Every Day Nature

A daily guide to the nature around you

Andy Beer

Every Day Nature

A daily guide to the nature around you

National Trust

In memory of John Sawyer and Lise Sinclair ...
... two wonderful people who, in very different ways,
helped me to learn how to notice things.

Published by National Trust Books
An imprint of HarperCollins Publishers
1 London Bridge Street
London SE1 9GF
www.harpercollins.co.uk

HarperCollins Publishers
Macken House, 39/40 Mayor Street Upper, Dublin 1, D01 C9W8, Ireland

First published 2020

ISBN 978-0-00883-622-1
10 9 8 7 6 5 4 3 2 1

A CIP catalogue record for this book is available from the British Library.

Printed and bound in India by Replika Press Pvt. Ltd.

If you would like to comment on any aspect of this book, please contact us at the above address or national.trust@harpercollins.co.uk

National Trust publications are available at National Trust shops or nationaltrustbooks.co.uk

The publishers would like to thank the following contributors for picture references: James at granthamecology.com for gorse, page 8 and Liz England at mywildlife.co.uk for dunnock, page 13.

MIX
Paper | Supporting responsible forestry
FSC™ C016779
FSC www.fsc.org

CONTENTS

INTRODUCTION

There is a common turn of phrase that turns up a lot in books about nature, which goes something like this: 'If you are really lucky then you may catch a glimpse of a bearded tit/otter/purple emperor butterfly' (delete as applicable).

I am sorry to break it to you, but no, you won't. What these books should say is: 'If you accompany an expert to exactly the place where these rare things are found, at exactly the right time of year – and you look where the expert is pointing – then you might have a chance of seeing the rear end of the creature in question as they fly away/dive under the water.'

I have been fascinated by nature for most of my life, but there are still lots of things I have never seen. So, this type of advice is not only discouraging, it also reinforces that sense that being interested in nature is simply a quest to fill in some long list, perhaps in the hope of a prize. There is always something brighter, rarer, more exciting just around the next corner.

Somehow nature has become the preserve of the experts. You have to appreciate it in a prescribed way, with the right equipment. You have to get the names right (don't call it a 'seagull'). You are required to dismiss some beautiful things because they are not native or invasive, which is ironic, given that just about everything that lives in this country had to invade after the ice last retreated fifteen thousand years ago.

This book is about another way to watch nature. It is about noticing the commonplace, marking the cycle of the seasons and taking time to study things closely. It's not about heading off to distant parts in order to find a creature; rather it is about looking at what is under your nose, and in writing this book I have had to spend time re-educating myself about the apparently simple business of 'how to see'.

The book is inspired by the work of an eighteenth-century vicar. Gilbert White's *The Natural History of Selborne* followed the turning of each year for more than two decades. Aside from time and a great sense of curiosity, the Reverend had the great advantage of not being distracted by rolling news from far away. So the eve of the declaration of American independence is greeted by an observation about the cherry-stealing habits of blackcaps. The storming of the Bastille passes him by while meditating on the habits of nightjars. I am not persuaded that he was much the poorer for it.

While writing, I too have ignored the news in favour of a daily dose of nature. It has reminded me how essential that is for my own wellbeing. Like many people, I find the descent into the dark days of winter saps my spirits and causes me to hunker down. The antidote is to notice things and take delight in them, to get as much fresh air as you can, stomp outside in the rain, go out on a freezing dark night.

We have somehow come to think of nature as something fragile that lives far away. Instead it is something huge and powerful that is all around us. If we take the time to slow down and observe, then the turning of the seasons can add great meaning to our lives. Looking at nature is also a helpful antidote to our own self-absorption. It reminds us that we live on a small island on the north-western fringe of a giant continent – many of the things we see in our gardens have travelled half the world to be here.

This book is meant as an inspiration to help you find and enjoy nature wherever you may live. It is not about the kind of nature that is restricted to nature reserves or remote places. Instead it is deliberately about things you will find in a garden, a park, a hedgerow or a road verge.

Expertise is not required; in fact it is overrated. You don't have to know exactly what something is called to appreciate it. Let me say that again: you don't have to know exactly what something is called to appreciate it. Curiosity and imagination are the currency of this book.

Notice a little bit of nature every day. It may change your life …

JANUARY

What is there to commend the month of January?

It can be a month of leaden skies and wild winds. Birds flock in gardens and field edges hunting for food and shelter. Bones of hawthorn hedges clatter in the winter breeze.

Yet, when the wind turns east, there can be glorious, crisp days with air so dry that it catches your breath and the crunch of a frozen puddle underfoot.

This is a time to appreciate the skeleton-spare beauty of winter, bark and branch, stone and soil.

Although it doesn't feel like it, we are imperceptibly tilting back towards the sun each day. If you look carefully enough, nature is beginning to waken.

Left: Gorse bushes.

1 JANUARY | NATURE WALK

We are in the depths of winter, but let me tell you the nature watcher's secret: spring starts in January. You have to look carefully, but as the year turns you can step outside and find something that tells you that the long nights are coming to an end and that the heat of the sun is slowly returning.

If you can watch a little bit of nature every day in January then the rest of the year is going to be a breeze. You have to work much harder to find nature in the winter, but that makes what is there all the sweeter.

So, today is the day to start as you mean to go on and force yourself outside for a breath of air as the rain pours and the wind howls. Walk, run, hop on a bike – whatever suits you – but get outside you must, even if it is just for a few minutes.

Keep your eyes open as you go: for although they are subtle, this month contains all sorts of little milestones that mark the turning of the year.

2 JANUARY | GOLDFINCH

I have a charm of goldfinches before me; clustered on a bird feeder, they are as charming as can be. It's hard to believe that these exotic birds, with heads of red, white and black and the brightest flash of gold on each wing, can just materialise in our gardens.

If you do nothing else this year then try to feed a goldfinch. This is the thistle finch, with a pointed beak for extracting tiny seeds from spiky flower heads. Goldfinches absolutely love little black niger seeds. Wherever you live, your feeder may bring you a finch one day.

News seems to travel fast among goldfinches. They are a constantly twittering gang, so advertising your feeder will not be necessary –

word of mouth (or beak) will suffice. In fact the word for a flock of goldfinches, a charm, derived from 'cirm' or 'cyrm', the Old English word for this twittering song.

3 JANUARY | GORSE FLOWER

It's said that you should kiss your beloved when the gorse is in flower. Happily, you could even find a flower now – on wasteland or a common or tucked in beside a wall – and the whole of the rest of the year too if you are so minded.

Even among the snow, the lemon-yellow flowers scatter the fringes of these dark, spiny bushes. Be warned though, they are fiercely prickly.

The gorse is the 'furze' of the Thomas Hardy novels; it burns hot and was used for cooking fires and bakeries. The furze cutters made a harsh living wrestling these spines – in *The Woodlanders* (1887) he writes, 'every individual was so involved in furze by his method of carrying that he appeared like a bush on legs'.

Remember where you found this flower and make a note to return on the hottest day of summer, when you can bathe in the coconut scent of gorse while listening to the seedpods cracking like fireworks in the heat.

4 JANUARY | VENUS

It is a clear evening and the evening star shines low in the western sky. Even in the city it is bright enough to see. It is often the first star to shine as the sky darkens; only the moon and sun are brighter.

But this is not a star at all, nor does it always appear in the evening. This is the strange, blue planet Venus. She does not deign to follow the stars as they wheel above. Instead, for nine months she follows the sunset as the 'evening star' and then disappears below the horizon for a month or two before reappearing for a spell of nine months as the 'morning star'. Named for the Roman goddess of beauty, love and fertility, she is our nearest neighbour, a hop and a skip of 25 million miles away if you time it right.

If you can hold binoculars still enough you can just see a tiny disc, not a point of light. Venus might be our neighbour, but she is nothing like our beautiful Earth. She is boiling hot, with carbon dioxide clouds and sulphuric acid for rain.

Make a point of bidding goodnight (or good morning) to our strange friend as she walks a unique path across our skies.

5 JANUARY | WASSAIL

Go and hang some toast in a tree. Go on, I dare you. If anyone mocks you then tell them proudly that you are upholding a great seasonal tradition.

Twelfth night is the night for wassailing – once unfairly described by a friend as 'dangerously close to folk music' – but in January, any excuse to get outside should be embraced.

If you can find a fruit tree then now is the time to scare off the evil spirits by making as much noise as you can and wishing for a blessed harvest. Or just breathe in the bracing winter air for a moment and clear your head. You can even take a drink with you, as that is part of the tradition too.

In this depth of winter it seems as if the dead trees will never wake again. They will, however, even without your blessing, but you will have to wait a few months yet.

6 JANUARY | DUNNOCK

Get to know a dunnock. One of the first things to do as you take an interest in nature is to get to know your resident birds in winter. Make friends with them now and they will keep you company for the rest of the year.

If you have ever watched a bird table you are likely to have seen a dunnock, but you may not have noticed it – like someone who hides in the kitchen at parties.

Be careful not to confuse him with a hedge sparrow (as some books do). This is a neat, insect-eating bird, not a raucous sparrow, and, despite appearances, it is not even in the sparrow family.

The dunnock's haunt is the ground and I much prefer their old name: the shufflewing. While other birds fight for the bird food on the table or hop among the trees, the shufflewing is quietly busy below, picking at the insects on the ground, steel-grey with a sparrow's brown back.

Once you have noticed them you will see them a lot, rarely flying far and full of character; marching to their own drum beneath the hedgerows.

7 JANUARY | EAST WIND

'Our Saxon forefathers called this month, with no small propriety, wolf month, because the severe weather brought down these ravenous beasts out of the woods among the villages'.

So wrote Gilbert White in January 1776 at a vicarage in Hampshire as he watched ice form on the inside of the windows.

In winter the east wind brings our weather straight from the Russian steppes, sometimes bright and clear, but more often a flat, grey sky with a flint wind that bites at your bones.

Unless you are a fan of rare birds, which this wind can sometimes bring but are not the subject of this book, I can think of little to commend the east wind in winter. Nonetheless it is a nature companion too. But for his taciturn company, we may treasure the south wind less.

8 JANUARY | YELLOW LICHEN

On a dark day the twigs of elder bushes are the brightest things in the grey winter scene. They are covered in yellow lichen, as if they have been dipped in oil paint.

Lichen is strange stuff; a combination of fungus with an algae or bacteria. This yellow lichen loves a small, rough twig, or a stone wall. It likes a bit of nitrogen pollution, too, so you are even more likely to see it in a town or near a farmyard.

This is the same lichen that grows by the sea, above the high-tide mark. It coats the roofs of St Ives, Cornwall, turning them yellow-orange, and this organism helped form part of the colour palette for Alfred Wallace and Patrick Heron of the St Ives School.

Be on the lookout for it – there is always room for a flash of yellow in your life.

9 JANUARY | WINTER MOTH

It's a bitter night and there is a moth on the window; small, triangular and drab with softly curved wings. I want to open the window and ask, 'What are you doing outside on a night like this, Mr Moth?'

This is a winter moth and I know how to address him, because the females are all but wingless. If you see a moth in the lamplight or fluttering in the car headlights then it will most likely be a winter moth. They occur right across the Northern Hemisphere and in some countries are abundant enough to be regarded as a pest. Here, though, they are much loved by blue tits to feed their first brood of chicks in the spring, so as far as I am concerned, the more of them there are the better.

10 JANUARY | WOLF MOON

Look at the moon in winter. If you can find a telescope then so much the better, but you don't really need one. We always see the same face of the moon, so you can become familiar with it. You can see craters with a pronounced white rim and great dark plains of basalt lava called 'seas'.

Recently we seem to have adopted the Native American habit of naming our full moons. The first moon of the year is the wolf moon, and I rather like the idea of howling at it – even if wolves no longer exist in the wild in the UK.

A full moon brings high 'spring tides'. It is not just a wonderful spectacle, but represents the huge force of nature on oceans across the world. That is something to make you feel incredibly small as you gaze upwards at the wonderfully named Sea of Tranquillity on our cold little satellite.

11 JANUARY | SHELTER

It's a wild day with the trees clattering together in the wind. On a day like this, it can seem as if the world has been emptied of all living things.

Today is the day to learn the value of shelter; that is where all of nature is hiding. Everything is tucked up in the midst of ivy-clad trees, among the heavy conifers or in the scruffy overgrown places that no one has thought to tidy up.

If you can find a sheltered spot then you might hear the chatter of birds. I once poked my head into a big ivy thicket and came face to face with a tawny owl (and nearly had a heart attack). Everything with any sense is tucked up somewhere.

Getting to know nature involves rewiring your mind. Tidy does not equal pretty; it often equals sterility. By contrast, untidiness is good: it may be the only place where something can survive when the weather turns fierce. For that reason it has a very particular type of beauty.

12 JANUARY | MOSS

Moss is amazing. It can grow on bare stone, bark or the poorest of soils. It stores water, provides homes for numerous insects. It is dogged, humble, soft and serene, yet on a misty morning it can sparkle with tiny droplets.

The Japanese know this: it is central to their gardens and their culture. A garden featuring moss-covered stone is highly prized – and indeed would be incomplete without it.

January is a good time to notice moss. It covers the interior of hedgerows and tucks into the cracks between roof tiles. If you can find a woodland stream then you may discover whole carpets of moss. If you look really closely, a patch of moss is like a miniature forest unfolding before your eyes.

Moss can even show you the way – it favours the north side of trees, where the sun cannot reach. Notice it, the plant of modesty and refinement.

13 JANUARY | LONG-TAILED TIT

There is no point going to look for a long-tailed tit. If they wish to visit you they will, but waiting for them is like watching a kettle coming to the boil.

However, if you feed the birds for long enough then you may be blessed with a visit from a squadron of long-tailed tits – much as the Red Arrows might drop by your village fête if they happen to be passing.

These are tiny, black-and-white birds, towing an improbably long tail like an advertising banner from a plane. They are quite beautiful and excel at aerobatics.

They are not rare, but they are definitely not something you can rely on. You might even see them along a road or by a hedgerow, but they do not turn up to order. You can often hear them coming as they career towards you, squeaking to each other to maintain close formation.

Once you see one, then you may see a dozen, invading the bird feeder in a big gang: the collective noun should be a *blessing* of long-tailed tits.

14 JANUARY | SNOWDROP

A January ritual is to find the place where the snowdrops grow: a garden, churchyard or a wood. Look closely and you will be rewarded with the sight of sharp, grey-green spikes poking through the grass and moss.

If you can hunt out a southern sunny bank or a light sandy soil then you may even greet the New Year with the flowering snowdrop. Here, on our cold clay soils, more patience is required.

Now all you need to do is imagine away a few weeks, when you will find woods carpeted with flowers as white as fresh fallen snow.

15 JANUARY | ROOTS

In January it sometimes feels as if nothing is growing. Everything is stuck and we are destined to live forever in a leafless landscape of short days and drear.

This isn't true for roots. As soon as the year turns, many roots start to grow beneath the ground, as long as the temperature is above freezing.

Roots have some remarkable chemistry that allows them to 'feel' their way in the dark, a little like when you get up in the night and navigate your way around without turning on the light. While all is still above, the roots of many plants are getting ready for the growth season to come.

16 JANUARY | WINTER ACONITE

This, for me, is the second flower of spring. It's a frequenter of churchyards, lagging a touch behind the snowdrop.

The bright yellow flowers emerge head first from the grass, towing a ruff of green leaves behind them. Like snowdrops they spread naturally into yellow drifts if left to their own devices.

One of winter aconite's local names is 'choirboys', referring to the ruff of green leaves that encircles the neck of the flower. They were introduced from southern Europe a long time ago and are enough to make you burst into song on a January morning.

17 JANUARY | BLUE TIT

How do you know a blue tit from the other birds? Answer: blue tits are the ones with the punk haircut. They look as if they have emerged from a teenager's bedroom after an ill-advised experiment with blue hair dye.

Blue tits will keep you company throughout the year, if you are kind enough to feed them. They are perky little birds that twitch to and fro and have a buzzy little call.

Once you get to know them they are not punkish at all. They are hardworking and mild, not minded to pick a fight when ousted from the bird feeder. That said, the one with the bluest hair has the best chance of getting the girl …

18 JANUARY | MALLARD

Ducks have a pretty rough time of it in my view. They get taken for granted for starters (and that is even before we mention duck decoys or orange sauce).

Don't take a mallard for granted. They might be the archetypal duck, the parent of countless domestic fowl, but they are stunningly beautiful wild birds.

The drakes have a shimmering green-blue head, white collar and beautiful grey back, and the brown females share the blue diamond flash under each wing.

Were they a rare bird, we would be celebrating their wondrous beauty and they would be pursued by people in camouflage with a spotting scope as soon as they appeared. It's funny that we don't notice their beauty simply because they are commonplace.

So, make amends and go and show them your appreciation. At this time of year you can be sure to find them on any lake or stream, where you will be able to watch them feed by upending themselves in the water, dabbling for food and showing a tail that is reminiscent of a Teddy boy haircut.

19 JANUARY | LAKE

If there is no nature in sight and you need a winter fix, then get yourself down to a lake or pond.

Unless it is frozen solid – and if so, this in itself is a reason for a visit – then a winter lake always has a little noise and life.

The intermittent quack, squeal and honk of birds on a winter lake has a sedate, calming air. Nothing seems to be in a rush. You might hear the whispers of reeds standing dead in the winter breeze, and perhaps the odd ripple of a fish.

The presence of water lifts the quality of the daylight even on the greyest day. This is nature watching with a zen air, soaking up a mood rather than looking closely. So wrap up warm, tune in and slow down. Make like a winter lake-dweller.

20 JANUARY | GHOSTING GNATS

Ghosts are stalking the park. There is just the faintest breath of heat from the January sun and a smoky haze of tiny insects is catching the light.

These are winter gnats and they really are a kind of ghost, feeding on dead and decaying plants and turning them into new life. Even in the depths of winter, you can see them on any day when the sun breaks through the clouds.

Tiny insects like these are to be treasured. Not only do they bring dying plants into new life, but they also provide a source of food for all sorts of larger creatures: beetle, bird or bat. They are barely noticeable, but in a low sun they dance like fireflies.

So, cherish that mass of dead leaves under the hedge and leave the stalks of last year's plants a while yet. Among the decay lies the prospect of resurrection – the seeds and eggs of new life.

21 JANUARY | PIED WAGTAIL

You will have seen a wagtail strutting somewhere around town. Their name is revealing as they constantly wag their long black-and-white tails while wandering across a verge or a car-park.

They are sharply dressed birds, somewhere between a pirate and a waiter – with a white face-mask and trim, monochrome jacket. They fly with a distinctive, looping style.

Pied wagtails seem to have taken to towns (perhaps because they are warmer places to roost at night). John Clare, the wonderful eighteenth-century poet, called them 'the little trotty wagtail' and he also noted their preference for a warm bed – 'your home is nigh at hand and in the warm pigsty.' I can't see one without thinking that it would be the friend that would slope off to a B&B when you were on a camping trip …

22 JANUARY | HAZEL CATKIN

The hazel trees on the edge of woods and in hedgerows and gardens are festooned with little kitten's tails. From a distance the pale yellow flowers look bright in the winter sun.

You can usually tell a hazel in winter by its shape. When cut it produces a flush of straight vertical shoots – good for walking sticks and pretend weapons for children.

This month no such observation skills are required; the catkins are all you need. We may not always think of trees as having flowers, but nearly all of them do. Every catkin on a hazel tree is a cluster of flowers, each hanging delicately from a silver-grey branch.

Hazel is a magical tree, said by the Celts to be the source of wisdom and inspiration. On a January day, an abundance of catkins is inspiration enough for me.

23 JANUARY | BLACKBIRD

Blackbirds are always reliable. In January they hang around on any patch of grass that they can find. The males are black with a yellow eye and the females a handsome brown.

This morning they are attacking an apple on the lawn. A bright yellow beak dives into the fruit's flesh while the other birds stand smartly around, watching like the doormen at a London hotel.

Most of our blackbirds are here year-round, so the chances are that these ones will be singing high on telephone wires later in the year, nesting in any quiet corner and screeching an alarm call if you get too close.

However, in winter they are also joined by some relatives from the Continent, so while I watch I like to speculate about which ones might be transient European visitors. If they are then they seem to rub along with the residents just fine.

24 JANUARY | HELLEBORE

If you have any space to grow anything at all, then please try to grow a hellebore. Anything that flowers in January is worth its weight in gold, even if it then does absolutely nothing else until the same time next year.

My hellebore is a deep purple, almost black, with creamy-coloured stamens in the nodding flower. It's quite improbable that such a huge and exotic bloom should appear at this time of year.

This plant is used to it, though – it comes from tough Alpine stock. I have seen a hellebore high up in the Corsican mountains, just beneath the snowline.

Our native green hellebore is a scarcer plant, found in ancient woods, but I suggest that you content yourself with one in the garden or in a pot so that you can relish the start of the spring flowering season from your window.

25 JANUARY | HOUSE SPARROW

I love sparrows in winter. If I go for a winter walk there is nothing better than stumbling across a gang of chattering sparrows hiding in a bush or mass of ivy. They are handsome too, patterned in brown, white and grey.

There is no quiet winter snooze for these birds. All is noisy and busy in the world of sparrows, like a New York taxi rank or a classroom when students are taking their seats.

Later in the year the sociable sparrows will all be finding a place to build some nests side by side, but for now they are scouting about for food, chirping gossip to each other as they go.

26 JANUARY | STARLING

Starlings make blackbirds look staid and sensible. At a distance they look quite similar, if slightly smaller. But, if you get a chance to see one close up in the right light, you will notice it has a coat of sequin-like spots.

You may see them coming to roost in a city at night, or hopping across fields among sheep in a busy group.

They are wonderful mimics. As a child I used to whistle at the rooftop starlings as I kicked a stone home from school – and they used to whistle right back.

At this time of year, if you can find the right place (a pier, certain towns or a reed-bed) you have the chance of seeing that wonder of wonders, a starling murmuration – thousands of birds gathering like smoke as the night closes in.

27 JANUARY | ALDER CATKIN

You will need to head to a waterway to find one of these: a lake edge, riverbank or canal towpath will do. Alders are common, but you might not have noticed them.

Alders are river trees, never happier than when their toes are in the water. If you can get close in January then you can find alder catkins, purple and tightly wrapped – clad in armadillo scales. You may also find the floating seeds from last year.

The buds and small twigs of the alder all share a damson-purple tinge. So get down to the riverbank where, in the right light, you can bathe in the purplish haze of a January alder tree.

28 JANUARY | ROBIN

Start the year by getting to know your neighbourhood robin. First, though, you must understand that you are in their neighbourhood. Robins are fiercely territorial birds, so it is likely that if you see a robin in the same place it will be the same bird.

Once you get over the fact that they are probably asking, 'What are you doing on my patch?' then you may be able to make friends.

Dig a hole, scuff up some ground, move a dustbin – and a robin may well appear hunting for dozy centipedes, worms or insects caught by surprise. Before you know it they will appear whenever you turn your back: a winter companion, sitting on top of your garden fork with a quizzical gaze.

29 JANUARY | MOLEHILL

Someone has been spring-cleaning … the grass is strewn with soft hillocks of soil, like someone has emptied buckets of earth to create a line of stepping stones across the damp turf.

If you stand among a collection of molehills you can imagine a huge underground network of tunnels inhabited by these industrious little creatures.

In an hour they can shift a hundred times their own weight in soil, and to do this they will eat up to half their body weight in worms every single day.

Moles are good soil scientists; their presence is a sign of high-quality, light, well-drained soil.

30 JANUARY | WOODLOUSE WORD CLOUD

gammer-zow · granny-picker · billy-button · carpenter · carpenter's flea · cheese-bug · cobber · hard-back · soda-pig · sow-pig · chissel-bob · chucky pig · cheese log · pellet bug · slaiter · cud-worm · palmer · lock-chester · tiggy-hog

31 JANUARY | WOODLOUSE

The variety of old names for woodlice tells you everything you need to know about these creatures that share our homes. One suspects that they moved in as soon as humans decided to put down roots and stay in one place.

We are the new kids on the block. Woodlice have been around for 350 million years and are one of nature's success stories. There are thousands of different species and they live in habitats that range from the edge of the seashore to the top of the highest mountain.

In my case, they live mainly in the log basket and, of course, in the shed. Miniature grey armadillos. Treasure them: modest human companions, completely harmless and tough as old boots.

FEBRUARY

February goes in fits and starts. On a still, sunny day, with your back to a southern wall, you may just imagine the breath of summer on your skin. On a day like this the insects start to appear, the birds sing and the buds visibly swell.

And then the wind turns and everything is put on hold – sometimes for weeks at a time.

Take heart from the fact that winter is losing its grip. Like a struggling heavyweight boxer, it can always catch you with a late punch, but the fight is only going one way from here.

Left: Fox and blackbird tracks in snow.

1 FEBRUARY | CROCUS

Crocuses appear overnight in the grass. Deep purple or bright yellow, they are the fleeting delight of this winter month.

Like many of our winter plants, crocuses grow wild high up in the mountains from Europe to Asia. They thrive on rocky Greek hillsides. The stamens of the autumn-flowering saffron crocus provide a product that is worth more than its weight in gold.

I think that the spring-flowering variety is valuable for a different reason. The leaves of the crocus will appear later, green and white spears – and if you want crocuses to spread then you will need to wait for them to die off before cutting the grass.

2 FEBRUARY | CANDLEMAS

It's another excuse to light a candle. I know that you should appreciate every moment, but I can't resist the temptation to count down the days during February, and today marks the traditional midpoint between the shortest day and the spring equinox.

Long before it was adopted as Candlemas, 2 February was regarded as one of the most significant days of the year. It's a reminder that so many of our annual rituals follow the cycle of the seasons.

I mark the day by planting some snowdrops, splitting big clumps into two and hoping for twice as many flowers next year, and occasionally buying a few new ones to add to the mix – now is the perfect time for snowdrop-planting.

3 FEBRUARY | GEOLOGY

There is a strange phenomenon in Arctic regions called patterned ground, which is caused by frost heaving stones to the surface as water collects beneath them, and then freezes and expands.

In parts of the UK a series of hard frosts will also lift stones to the surface of the soil, so this time of year is a really good time to get to know the geology of where you live.

The type of rock and the pH of the soil play a big part in defining what nature you are going to see. Dry or wet, acid, neutral or alkaline, the soil determines the mixture of plants that will thrive and thus many of the insects and birds that feed on them.

Either way, it is easy to find out what soil you have, and it helps to know so you can go hunting for lime-loving plants on a chalky hill, or reptiles on a sandy heath. Luckily we live in a country where you can often move from one soil type to another within a mile or two, so you will often get the best of both worlds.

4 FEBRUARY | SCRUB

One of my favourite nature sightings was the report of a nightingale in the bushes at Reading services on the M4 motorway. We may not have heard it sing but it was a reminder to us all about the neglected value of scrub.

Scrub is what you find on waste ground, in the field margins, the railway line or tip. It's an in-between thing. It doesn't fit into the neat boxes that we like to apply. It's not neat and straight enough for a hedge and certainly not statuesque enough to be called 'woodland'. If you don't fit in then you get overlooked.

You don't have to take the same view. If you can find a patch of scrub on a February day it is a great place to be. Within its protection you may find the first spring leaves or a sheltering bird. That nightingale was singing us a lesson about the errors of tidiness. Far from being commonplace and unimportant, it turns out that 'in-between' spaces – grassland with thorns; edges and fringes – are some of the most important of all.

5 FEBRUARY | CELANDINE

'And the first moment that the sun may shine, bright as the sun himself, 'tis out again!' wrote Wordsworth in 'A Lesson' of the little many-petalled celandine, one of the earliest flowers to carpet a hedge bank with 'scalloped splashes of gold'.

Celandines are hard to mistake for anything else and easy to love. Their petals are glossy yellow, as if painted with nail varnish. They sit just above dark, kidney-shaped leaves. The flowers spread readily in shady woods, gardens and hedge banks. True to the poem, they open fully at the slightest hint of sunshine.

6 FEBRUARY | MAGPIE

Magpies are unmistakable. They are large, truculent crows with a long tail and an iridescent, green-purple sheen on their black-and-white feathers.

I once spent a few days on a farm where the family had a pet magpie that was convinced that it was a dog: it barked when you approached and slept with its stepbrother in the dog basket.

Some think magpies unlucky, at least when seen singly. I prefer to mutter, 'One for sorrow, two for joy' and hope for a pair. They are much persecuted as farmland pests – but you cannot deny that they are beautiful nonetheless.

7 FEBRUARY | FOOD WEBS

Imaginary letter to the editor: 'How can you write a nature book that praises magpies? There are far too many of them. They are cruel scavengers that eat young songbirds and eggs. What kind of bird is this to celebrate?'

This is true, of course: magpies are certainly thriving and their abundance may well be a symptom of man's influence on the landscape.

But let's start at the beginning, shall we? There is an awkward truth about nature that you need to reconcile yourself with to help you love it. Whisper it quietly, 'Everything eats everything else …'

The food web (the technical term) that sustains even the smallest garden is incredibly complex: wasps and flies laying eggs inside the larvae of caterpillars, moths tricking other insects to foster their young, fungi cutting deals with tree roots to exchange scarce minerals for sugars, and so it goes on.

So, don't pick on the predators and scavengers – everyone is at it. The key thing is to make sure that there is enough to eat for all. That means choosing to treasure the whole circular system, rather than seeing demons where there are none.

8 FEBRUARY | WOOD PIGEON

The wood pigeons in my neck of the woods seem to sing 'I don't know, Nigel' in a cooing, dolorous fashion.

Theirs is the first bird song to learn – nice and easy, but comforting in its own way. Familiarise yourself with it now and you won't mistake it for a cuckoo if you are lucky enough to hear one later in the spring.

We tend to be dismissive of pigeons, which is odd, because the inhabitants of south-west France revere them highly and hunt them obsessively as soon as autumn arrives. There the wood pigeon or *palombe* is the gourmet's delight.

True wood pigeons are a beautiful slate grey with a white splash across their neck. Even if eating them is not your preference, we could all learn from the French in showing them due appreciation.

9 FEBRUARY | RED KITE

Surely a red kite is not commonplace enough for a book like this?

Well, they just might be. Since the few surviving Welsh kites were joined by some reintroduced birds in 1989, they have prospered and spread and they are really hard to miss – most likely circling above a motorway or catching a thermal on a hillside.

They are huge hawks, red-winged with grey elbow patches, and they fly in a lazy, lugubrious way – as though it is too easy for them and they can't really be bothered.

If you can get a good view then they are easy to tell apart from any other bird of prey by the clear V-shaped notch in their tail, which twitches and tilts left and right like the rudder of an aeroplane.

Their laid-back attitude is reflected in their chosen diet, hunting around for dead animals, roadkill and perhaps the odd earthworm.

So, you don't even need to worry about your garden birds or your pet rabbit – red kites are not really designed or minded to chase and kill things.

10 FEBRUARY | PRIMROSE

I have a distant memory of gathering posies of primroses in a Kentish wood and have, somewhere, a black-and-white photograph of me clutching the most perfect bunch. Prima facie evidence for what is now considered a misdemeanour.

Primroses are creamy yellow with fat green leaves, one of the first spring flowers of woodland and hedgerow bank. They were Benjamin Disraeli's favourite flower – common on the Chilterns around his Buckinghamshire country retreat, Hughenden.

Plant breeders have created all sorts of multicoloured varieties of *Primula* (the Latin name for primrose). I don't know why really, because none of them are a patch on the original species, *Primula vulgaris*. Notice them, plant one, buy one for Valentine's Day – but don't pass them by.

11 FEBRUARY | CONKER BUD

It's too cold and breezy for wildlife. Everything is hunkered down.

So, today is a day for noticing tree buds. They start to swell at this time of year and when the dog of winter growls again – as it is wont to do in February – a tree bud is a good reminder that the hound will soon be cowering before the summer sun.

Tree buds all look the same, don't they? But look closer and you will see ash (black and soot-like), or maybe beech (sharp, brown and pointed).

If you can find one, though, the horse chestnut (our conker tree) is the most distinctive of all. They are acorn-sized, with a sharp point, and are sticky to the touch. You may return during summer to see the white candelabra flowers, and in autumn for some deep brown conkers, but in February you will have to imagine all of that promise contained within a sticky bud.

12 FEBRUARY | LEYLAND CYPRESS

This is the much-derided garden hedge plant, *Cupressus × leylandii*, the subject of lawsuits and disputes, but a great place for birds to shelter in February. It deserves a little more love for that alone and if you delve inside one you may well find an old wren or blackbird nest making use of the dense cover.

The tree itself is a cross between two American trees that live half a continent apart, but which happened to meet in the garden at Leighton Hall in Powys, Wales. Their offspring is the fast-growing hybrid tree that populates suburban gardens everywhere.

They are not a great choice for a garden hedge and look scruffy as soon as you have pruned them. But I can't look at one without thinking of their parent trees; one perched beside a shimmering bay in southern California and the other towering over the black water lying off the coast of Vancouver Island.

13 FEBRUARY | CHAFFINCH

The song of a chaffinch is like a village cricketer running up to bowl; a trundling approach followed by an explosion of whirling arms and legs.

Although it is one of the earliest spring songs, I don't think it's an easy one to learn. So, I suggest that you learn the birds by sight first and save the song for another year.

Fortunately, male chaffinches are easy to spot, with a bright blue head and orange breast. Female chaffinches look a bit like sparrows, with white flashes on their wings.

Chaffinches have a penchant for hanging around picnic tables and picking scraps of cake from under your feet – which means that you can combine your nature-watching with a hot cup of tea and a flapjack.

14 FEBRUARY | VALENTINE'S DAY

Confession time: I have never really understood Valentine's Day. Red roses in February? There is definitely something not right about that.

That said, the birds and mammals have definitely got the message. Blackbirds and chaffinches are tearing around in pursuit of one another. No prizes will be awarded for subtlety, but persistence is almost as good.

In the churchyard the tawny owl will have already nested, and the blackbirds and others will soon follow suit. If you want to help some newly-wed birds then now is a great time to put up a nest box.

I suppose I shall just have to succumb to the forces of the season, cook dinner and cut some hellebores from the garden while they are still looking fine.

15 FEBRUARY | EARTHWORM

It's time to get a spade out and check on the earthworms. As a rule of thumb, a healthy spadeful of soil should contain at least ten worms.

This is not a trivial matter. Charles Darwin wrote in his final book that 'nobody and nothing can be compared with earthworms in their positive influence on the whole living Nature'.

It takes a thousand years to make an inch of soil. Earthworms do most of the work, pulling vegetation into the ground, digesting it and aerating the soil with their burrows. They like nothing more than a pile of mulch on a spring flower bed.

If you look after the earthworms, a lot of the nature will come to you. Thrushes love them, moles survive on them and the soil that they create is teeming with life – a teaspoon of healthy soil contains millions of different living things.

16 FEBRUARY | HERRING GULL

In winter you can find gulls wheeling in a leaden sky. Birds of the wild ocean, found adrift in a city or on a ploughed winter field. It's a kind of miracle that a bird of such wilderness should make its home with us.

If you see a gull over a field or a waste tip, it is most likely a herring gull. Herring gulls are huge, with a strong, yellow bill and pink feet. Their song is the sound of a British seaside town: wailing, brassy and loud.

They are clever, adaptable scavengers. Some think of them as cruel and base, but you don't have to make this choice.

Coastal people once saw them as friends and gulls now coexist with town and country dwellers too. When I see one, I like to think of the fishermen who used them to locate herring shoals, in the days when the oceans ran silver with fish.

17 FEBRUARY | SNOW TRACKS

At some point in February you may get a dusting of snow. Or you may get a whole heap of it. Either way, this is a time to jump out of bed and get outside before anyone else.

You might think that where you live there isn't much wildlife about. Now go for a short walk and look at the tracks in the snow. The base of any hedge or shrub will be marked with the tracks of birds. You will probably be able to see the prints of a lone fox over any patch of open ground. In other places you will see all too clearly that, while you were asleep, you missed a serious party.

My favourite are rabbit prints – two big hind feet and two small front feet – as if two ill-matched people have joined together to make a cunicular pantomime horse.

18 FEBRUARY

BLACKTHORN FLOWER

These are the first of the hedgerow flowers, emerging from a spiny, steel-black stem of the plant that, along with hawthorn, is the staple of our hedgerows. The first blackthorn flower is a modest thing, but it signals that the hedge is awakening: creamy-white petals in a five-pointed star, about the size of a penny.

The blackthorn is a plum tree, and before too long it will be covered in blossom. Even later in the year, you may come back looking for ingredients for Christmas sloe gin, but for now you will have to make do with a single, perfect flower.

19 FEBRUARY | ROOKERY

Watch out for a rook carrying a stick – the harbinger of spring. The rook in question will be on its way back to the rookery for a bit of nest-building.

You probably have a rookery near you. High up in the treetops, rooks make colonies of big, scruffy nests, sometimes 30 or more.

Rooks are clever and sociable. They have a bare patch of greyish skin at the base of their beaks, which makes them look a bit quizzical. They mainly eat worms and grubs and they make their homes in the same places year after year. Some rookery sites are more than a hundred years old.

February is time for some serious rookery refurbishment, to get ready for the nesting season. They are busy, practical and, I like to think, optimistic birds. For that reason, a February sighting of a rook carrying a stick, even on the greyest of days, always makes me smile.

20 FEBRUARY | OAK APPLE

Keep an eye out on the trees for oak apples and the similar oak marble gall – fake fruit for a February day. It's pretty hard to identify an oak tree in winter, but an oak apple is absolutely distinctive – usually attached to a smaller branch, about the size of a gobstopper.

These galls are caused by small parasitic wasps and represent just two of around 80 different types of gall that form on oak. They may well have a hole in them where the larva has chewed its way out. Oak apples are not just home to a single type of wasp. On the contrary, they are the setting for a vicious turf war between insects who want to lay their own eggs in the gall and parasites who want to inject their eggs into the larvae.

Oak galls were also once the major ingredient of ink for writing. The distant cousins of the gall on the twig in front of you provided the ink for Magna Carta.

21 FEBRUARY | WOODPECKER DRUM

Listen out for the drum of a woodpecker. At this time of year our great spotted woodpeckers start to busy themselves.

If you hear a quick hammering sound in the distance then it is almost certainly a great spotted woodpecker. You may not see one, but they are found almost anywhere with large trees.

The pitch of a woodpecker drum depends on the size and hollowness of the tree. If you keep your eyes peeled on dead trees then you might even spot a woodpecker hole that is all ready for nesting in spring – just large enough for a sleek black-and-white bird to squeeze inside.

22 FEBRUARY | DOG'S MERCURY

This is one of the first woodland plants to appear. It quickly covers the base of hedgerows and the woodland floor in February.

It grows shin-high and is the most ordinary and unprepossessing of plants. It's easier to recognise once it has burst forth into flower – in the most modest of ways – with a tiny vertical spike adorned with miniature green circular flowers. And it's poisonous.

In summary, there is not much to commend it. It's a backdrop plant, setting off the showy ones around it, yet it is named after Mercury, the messenger of the Gods. Maybe the message is that modesty is underrated.

23 FEBRUARY | JACKDAW FLIGHT

The winter skies are punctuated with ragged groups of crows, skittering in the breeze like ashes from a paper fire.

The squeaky-toy call of 'jack, jack' is the giveaway. This is a gathering, a 'clattering' of jackdaws. They are actually really good at flying, but I like to think they just mess about whenever the mood takes them. It certainly seems that way.

Jackdaws are one of our smallest crows. They famously have an eye for a shiny thing – a grey-hooded jewel thief of a bird.

24 FEBRUARY | GREAT TIT

Listen for a great tit. Winter is a great time to get to know your birds and great tits are one of the first to start singing to attract a mate.

They have a repetitive, mechanical song, like a wheelbarrow with a squeaky wheel. 'Teacher, teacher', they shout from any available perch.

I always think that great tits are a bit smarter than blue tits – with a black stripe down their yellow front as if they have put on a tie with their green-jacketed wings.

Later on in the year – but not too much later – they will be scouting around for a place to nest, but for now you will most likely see them perched high up in the trees showing off madly.

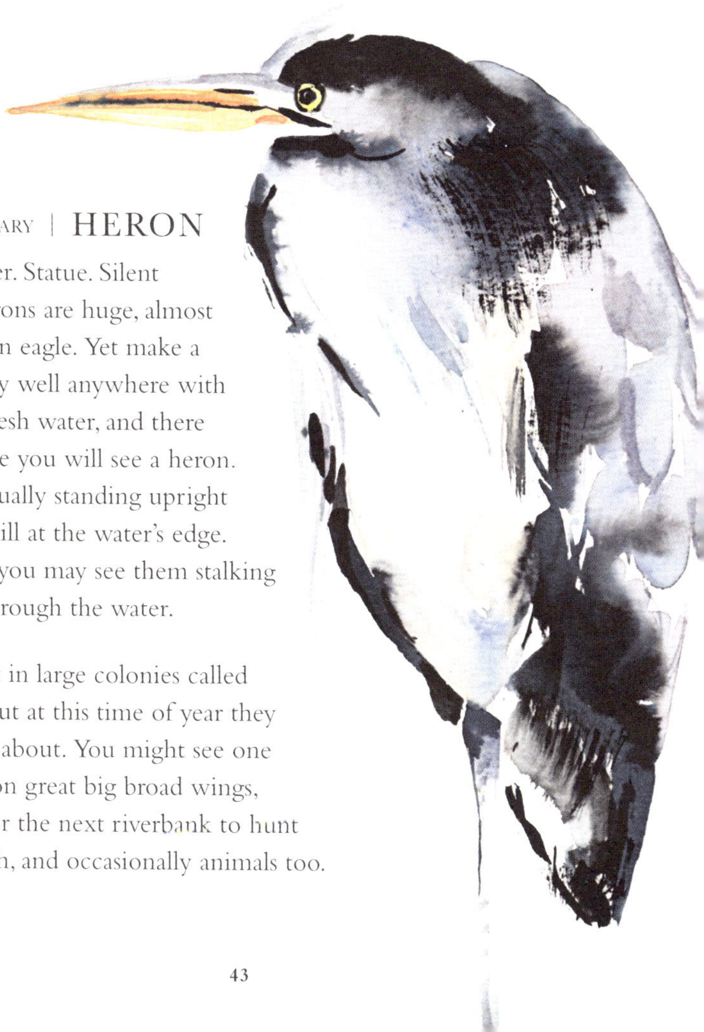

25 FEBRUARY | HERON

Pond dweller. Statue. Silent assassin. Herons are huge, almost the size of an eagle. Yet make a trip to pretty well anywhere with a body of fresh water, and there is the chance you will see a heron. They are usually standing upright and stock-still at the water's edge. Sometimes you may see them stalking on tiptoe through the water.

They nest in large colonies called heronries, but at this time of year they are out and about. You might see one flying past on great big broad wings, searching for the next riverbank to hunt for small fish, and occasionally animals too.

26 FEBRUARY | ARUM LEAF

Under the hedges and beside the pavements, there are bright green, arrow-shaped leaves, almost as large as your hand.

This is the most extraordinary plant: it transmutes into a strange flower and then once again into a red-berried spike. *Arum maculatum* goes by several other names too: cuckoo pint, lords and ladies, devil's pightle, to name but a few.

Arum derives from the Arabic word for 'fire', and it is said that eating the leaves causes a burning sensation, though I would not recommend that you try it.

Note where you see the leaves and come back in a couple of months to see the next strange incarnation.

27 FEBRUARY | RIVERBANK

'All water … holds memory and the space to think.' (Roger Deakin, quoted in *Landmarks*, Robert Macfarlane, 2015.)

February is a good time to wander along a riverbank and make friends with a river. There is warmth and shelter here and that means there will be signs of life in this cold season. Last year's dead vegetation strews the bankside and makes a home for insect larvae, voles and shrews.

Your river might slink calmly through the reeds, or gush over rocks. It may be the shallowest of streams. Best of all is a few days after a winter storm, when the rivers burst over into floodplains and turn the world into a giant, temporary waterscape.

Ripple and rock, ruffle and rill: rivers bring movement and sound into the winter air. There is no better time for a meditative stroll along the bank.

28 FEBRUARY | RIVER NAMES

Aeron · Afton · Aire · Allan · Arrow · Avon · Axe · Bann · Beal · Brue · Calder · Cherwell · Churn · Churnet · Clyde · Cole · Dart · Dee · Eden · Evenlode · Exe · Frome · Glyme · Hart · Itchen · Isis · Kennet · Kent · Lark · Lyn · Medina · Mersey · Nadder · Nene · Nevis · Nidd · Ouse · Rhondda · Severn · Silver · Spey · Stour · Tamar · Tavy · Tay · Thames · Torridge · Trent · Tyne · Valency · Wye · Wylye · Windrush

29 FEBRUARY | HOAR FROST

A bright hoar-frost morning is a wondrous thing.

Here you have a choice: you can complain about having to scrape the windscreen of your car, or you can take a minute to stop and soak up a world transformed by tiny crystals of ice, while watching your breath make clouds in the morning sun.

In February a sharp frost feels like a cleansing thing. It breaks the soil into crumbs and kills off unwanted pests. Our native plants are adapted to frost, as long as it is not too late in the season. If it goes on for a day or two then you will need to remember to put some water out for the birds, but today you may just enjoy a frozen land.

MARCH

'The hard blue winds of March shake the young
sheep and flake the long stone walls …'
(From 'The Three Winds', Laurie Lee, 1989)

It seems that all the seasons take place during March. At the beginning of the month you can bask in summer warmth on one day and freeze in biting sleet the next. Nonetheless, it is the season for mating and nesting, for flowering and growth.

March is for blossom-clad verges and tadpoles in ponds. Turn your back and plants appear. Listen well and the air is abuzz again.

Left: Bullfinches eating cherry blossom.

1 MARCH | DAFFODIL

It is Daffodil Day, or St David's Day if you prefer, and the daffodil display is in full cry.

In a few parts of the country the woodland floor is carpeted with wild daffodils, small and delicate, two-tone yellow beneath the straight, brown stems of hazel or the cracked bark of oak.

It was the wild variety, *Narcissus pseudonarcissus*, which stimulated Wordsworth's raptures about daffodils, but there is no need to be choosy: from pale white narcissus to brash yellow, daffodils shout spring with glorious abandon.

2 MARCH | HARE

The hare – swift and sacred animal. Creature of March and myth, symbol of fertility and the original and best Easter bunny.

They are not common, but if there is ever a moment to see one then now is the time. Unlike rabbits they favour a ploughed field. At this time of year I look at every field of spring crops, hoping that each clump of grass or low pile of weeds might be a crouching hare.

By late April, the barley will have grown too tall to see them, but during March you may even see them chasing each other around at high speed.

Black-tipped ears, huge, long back legs and wild eyes – if you are lucky enough to spot one it is an encounter with something ancient.

3 MARCH | RED DEAD-NETTLE

This plant is not really red (more purple), it is not dead and it doesn't sting like a nettle. They are a plant of scruffy places, field edges, roundabouts and verges that have just been dug up.

But … they flower early and at this time of year they are beloved of the first bees, providing much-needed food as they wake from the winter. March is when you notice them, popping up, as often as not, among dandelions and dock leaves.

It's said that you can eat them too, but I have never felt the urge or necessity. Leave them for the bees, I say – and perhaps delay your first cut of grass until there are other sources of nectar on offer.

4 MARCH | LARCH BUD

Did you know that not all conifers are evergreen? Larch is our only widespread conifer tree that sheds its needles over winter.

At this time of year the new growth appears, and it is worth a closer look at the lower branches. The new needles burst from the stems like tiny green versions of my grandfather's shaving brush. Beneath them you may also find shocking-pink larch flowers.

They are fine timber trees too. They were favoured as a 'nurse crop' for other trees as they grow rapidly, suppress weeds and don't cast much shade. They also produce terrific light, weatherproof wood much used for fencing and sheds.

I think that the flowers are amazing. Once you see them, you can't help but think, 'Why have I never noticed that before?'

5 MARCH | FROGSPAWN

This year, finally, I am going to get round to constructing a pond. Nothing fancy, but a patch of water to bring more life to the garden. At this time of year, even the tiniest ponds suddenly fill with great, gelatinous clumps of frogspawn, or long threads of draping toadspawn.

Ponds definitely obey the *Field of Dreams* principle of nature – 'If you build it, they will come.' That is reason enough to establish one of your own. Even the smallest patch of water will be found by a frog or a toad as quick as a flash.

If you have still water nearby, take a torch out at night and have a look – you may be greeted by the strange sight of protruding eyes staring back at you from just above the waterline.

6 MARCH | NESTING

The birds have one thing in mind at this time of year, and that is nesting. Watch out though, because anything soft and fluffy that you leave lying around may well be repurposed as lining – and if you watch closely then you will see birds on the hunt for the perfect material.

Much like the three little pigs, birds have distinct preferences when it comes to building materials: some favour sticks (wood pigeons and rooks); others prefer mud (song thrushes, house martins); and then there is the moss crowd (long-tailed tits, for example).

Others have more exotic tastes. Once, while rooting around a scrapyard in an attempt to keep one of our old family cars going, my father found a chaffinch nest constructed entirely from copper wire taken from the broken alternator of an old Morris Minor: a perfect woven golden jewel.

7 MARCH | BLACKBIRD CHORUS

Suddenly the evenings start to lengthen. The sun slows imperceptibly towards sunset, offering a glimpse of the endless evenings of the northern latitudes to come. And the blackbirds know it first.

If there is warmth in the evening air then now is the time to get outside. Put on another layer, prick up your ears and settle in.

In the half hour after sunset, the chorus commences.

Blackbirds. Perched as high as they can, filling the spring evening with song.

The dawn chorus may be amazing, but it takes some effort to get up for that. The blackbird chorus, by contrast, involves finding a place with a few tall trees and standing outside with an early evening drink in your hand.

8 MARCH | VIOLET

'March 8, 1783. The air is soft. Violets blow. Snow lies under the hedges. Men plow.'

Keep your eyes open, and just like Gilbert White you will see some violets, perhaps on an old, short mown lawn, a verge or in a hedgerow. If you have no luck then try an old piece of woodland instead.

In among the purple, you will find patches of white violets too, all with the same flowers that look vaguely inverted.

There are numerous variants of violet. Sweet violet (*Viola odorata*) is beautifully scented, whereas the dog violet (*V. riviniana*) is without scent. The smell of some violets can be elusive; a major component is a chemical that temporarily desensitises the receptors in the nose. Certainly, I can never catch more than the most fleeting hint of the perfume of violets. You may have a better sense of smell than me, although you are likely to attract curious glances if you spend too long kneeling on the woodland floor trying to tell which species you have found.

9 MARCH | QUEEN WASP

Big, dozy wasps are on the move. At this time of year, they will most likely be queen wasps, off to found a new colony. You will see them hungrily perched on the early flowers, building up their strength after a winter sleep.

Before too long you might spot wasps perched on fences, sheds and posts, stripping off thin layers of wood to make a complex, hexagon-celled nest: one of the wonders of nature.

We seem to love bees despite their sting, but hate wasps. Maybe it's because they can sting us several times and survive – whereas one can't help but feel more sympathy for a bee that has been roused to suicidal anger.

10 MARCH | SONG THRUSH

In among the blackbirds you may see a handsome song thrush. Like blackbirds, they prefer to perch in the treetops to sing out their territory, but unlike their cousins they sing in a pattern of (usually three) identical repeated phrases.

You have to listen for a little while, but once you tune into the pattern you can pick the song out from the crowd. You can tell the birds by their spotted breasts and pale brown back.

In addition to the serenade, if you are really lucky, then your local thrush might decide to use a nearby step as an anvil for its favourite sport: snail-smashing. They don't bother to hide the evidence.

11 March | CHIFFCHAFF

Every spring we are joined again by a host of summer birds from the south, flying across continents and oceans to raise a family here.

For me, the chiffchaff is usually the first arrival and each year I listen for it as soon as March sweeps in.

Remember the 'teacher, teacher' song of the great tit? This is a similar two-note call – but less of a squeaky wheel and more like a blacksmith hammering two ends of an anvil. The bird is named after its call.

This is the first of the cascade of new songs that only ends when the swifts arrive in May, and if you can begin to notice some of them, they will forever mark the season for you.

You may well not see it – a little green-brown leaf warbler with a pale eye-stripe, flitting around in the higher branches – but the song is the thing: 'I'm back, I'm back'.

12 March | BLACKTHORN BLOSSOM

From a single flower in February to a foam of blackthorn white lining every lane and main road in March.

Blackthorn spreads out to form a triangular clump and at this time of year the leafless, steel-black stems are covered in flowers.

How do you tell our two common hedgerow plants apart? Simple: with blackthorn the flowers appear before the leaves; while with hawthorn the leaves come before the flowers. Wait for a warm day and seek out a south-facing bank of flowering thorn. When you get close you will hear the summer hum of insects in the sunshine.

Bee, wasp, fly and hoverfly create a symphony of high-pitched tones. It's enough to make you want to plunge your head into the flowers as well – although a crown of thorns will surely follow if you succumb to the temptation.

13 MARCH | RED-TAILED BUMBLE BEE

The queen red-tailed bumble bees are one of the first to be up and about in the spring. You might even see them in February, but you have a good chance from early March. Needless to say they are black with a red tail, which fades to almost white as the summer proceeds.

Just like the honey bee, bumble bees are social creatures. They make their nests in holes in the ground, under sheds or walls. You can get quite close – bumble bees very rarely sting – and it is lovely to watch them animate a spring flower bed.

14 MARCH | DANDELION

Taste is one of the best ways to remember things. If you have ever picked a dandelion and licked your fingers then you will know what I mean. The bitter-tasting white sap borne on its hollow stem creates a memory that lasts a lifetime.

You can eat the leaves in salads, make wine from the flowers and medicinal tea from the roots, which acts as a diuretic. But that is all too practical. Dandelions are yellower than the lion for which they are named. They are so soft that when massed together you imagine that you could cushion yourself on their blooms.

Edible, curative, memorable, beautiful and soft as silk: what more could you want from a flower?

15 MARCH | PETTY SPURGE

On the edge of the pavement is a little spurge plant. It has strange, green flowers in trios on a green 'leaf'. Don't pass it by, it is worth a second look.

This is one of our native *Euphorbia* plants and you will notice its similarity to all the big garden euphorbias with acid-green flowers that are out at this time of year.

The stems exude a sap that can irritate your skin, but it also has some positive uses and has long been known as a medicinal plant, as a treatment for skin complaints, asthma, catarrh and diarrhoea. This little weed is part of a family with thousands of members (around 4,000 species known worldwide) – all named, believe it or not, after the Greek doctor to the King of Mauritania, Euphorbus.

16 MARCH | PUSSY WILLOW

If you get down by the water then you might be able to find a sallow tree breaking into flower. Sallow loves having wet feet and the two different types, *Salix caprea* and *Salix cinerea*, are commonplace by rivers and ditches.

At this time of year, the flower buds are covered in the softest grey fur: half tree, half cat. If you cut a branch or two and put them in water then you can watch them burst into pale yellow flowers.

All sorts of lovely moths depend on sallow trees, but it is also the food plant of what Matthew Oates calls 'His Imperial Majesty' (*In Pursuit of Butterflies*, 2015), the Purple Emperor – the most spectacular of all British butterflies. It's also among the rarest, so I cannot promise you a sighting of one of those, I am afraid.

17 MARCH | BRIMSTONE

Big and butter-yellow: the first butterfly of spring and the first butterfly anyone should learn.

If you can feel the warmth of the sun in March then chances are you might see a brimstone. It is the only yellow butterfly that you will see at this time of year so you can't make a mistake.

Close up it is almost leaf-shaped, but you probably won't be able to get too near unless you are minded to do some serious butterfly-chasing, as they don't tend to settle very often.

If it is your first, then write down the date and mark it on next year's calendar. This, forever, is your brimstone day.

18 MARCH | CHERRY BLOSSOM

In Japan, the arrival of cherry blossom sparks a fortnight-long celebration of picnics and parties.

I think we have something to learn. For centuries, the arrival of the blossom has been marked by the custom of *hanami* – taking a drink beneath a cherry tree.

Flowering cherries range from pure white to deep pink and they often don't produce fruit. The blossom is perfect for just a few days: less if the wind and rain is timed badly. It is both miraculous and ephemeral.

Somewhere, on the way to work, in a garden or a square, will be a cherry tree for you to notice and adopt. If you are lucky you might find a whole street full of them. Either way, make sure to offer a small toast as you pass them by.

19 MARCH | LEAFING HAWTHORN

'Tired of his northern tune, the winds turn soft, blowing white butterflies out of the dog rose hedges …' ('The Three Winds', Laurie Lee, 1989.)

Sooner or later you will get a balmy March day, I promise.

The hedgerows will have been pretty stark until now, but hawthorn is usually the first to break into leaf, and it happens quickly as soon as the air warms up.

Hawthorn is the ultimate hedging tree. It is thorny, thick and vigorous and will soon be a haven for numerous nests. You can eat the young leaves as a salad vegetable; an old forester friend would always pick a few to go in his cheese sandwiches.

20 MARCH | VERNAL EQUINOX

The spring equinox is one of the days that marks the turning of the year. Today, the day and the night are exactly equal in length. Tomorrow the light starts to win out.

Equinox is a special day for us, but the plants notice the change too. That's because quite a few of them have the ability to tell the time. The length of the day, or more accurately, the length of the night, is one of the things that determines when many plants start to grow or flower.

Temperature matters too, of course, but for some plants this ability to tell the time – known as photoperiodism – sets the pattern of their lives.

It's a big day and we should mark it too – time for a spring clean, I think.

21 MARCH | BULLFINCH

I think that these are the smartest of all the finches, but they are not a species that you are guaranteed to see. They are bright rose-red with a smart black cap.

If ever there is a chance to see one then now is the time. Listen out for a couple of low whistles, and keep watch high up in the hedgerows or fruit trees, and there you may see bullfinches methodically eating fresh flowering buds.

At one time fruit farmers used to trap bullfinches, and as recently as the 1950s some fruit farms trapped more than a thousand birds. This is the kind of environmental problem that we could do with – a surfeit of bullfinches.

22 MARCH | CUCKOO FLOWER

'When daisies pied and violets blue
And lady-smocks all silver-white
And cuckoo-buds of yellow hue
Do paint the meadows with delight'
(from *Love's Labour's Lost*, William Shakespeare, 1598)

It's a bit early for cuckoos but not too early for the cuckoo flower, at least in sheltered places.

This is the most delicate plant of damp meadows, but it crops up alongside pavements and in gardens too.

The cuckoo flower has fine, pale pink flowers with four petals, poking out above the grass on a slim stem, and they also go by the name of lady's smock.

For me though, they will always be 'milkmaids', the Kentish name that my mother taught me.

23 MARCH | WILD GARLIC

You will need a trip to the woods for this one. In the right place – a damp, shady, lime-rich woodland – wild garlic can cover the whole forest floor. Here the scent of garlic smacks you in the face, like a loving Gallic embrace.

Big, green garlic leaves coat the woodland floor like the plates on the back of a dinosaur. Later, the white globular flowers shatter the scene like a spring hailstorm.

The leaves are beloved of smart restaurants. Personally, I choose to leave them be – I can never bear to disrupt the perfection of a March spring woodland floor. Breathing in the aroma is quite enough for me.

24 MARCH | FORSYTHIA

One of the pitfalls of getting to know nature is that there is a risk of falling into ascetic tendencies – no sooner do you start to appreciate something than you start to find reasons to deny yourself part of it.

One of the manifestations of this is a refusal by some to assign value to anything that is not native – even though it may be beautiful. That seems a bit miserable to me, not to mention increasingly hard to justify as we start to adapt to a changing climate.

Watch out for this tendency creeping up on you and today, as an antidote, enjoy the beauty of common-or-garden forsythia: one of the earliest plants to reach our gardens from the Far East, bright yellow, blowsy and glorious on a showery spring afternoon.

25 MARCH | TOAD

I once spent a year living in a tiny rented house by a river. When travelling home on a rainy night, I was confronted by an impenetrable roadblock. Or, to be more accurate, a 'toadblock', as the whole road was carpeted with toads. There was nothing else to be done but abandon the car and tiptoe, coatless, gently home.

At this time of year toads are on the move, answering an ancient call to migrate. In the first rainstorm after a dry spell, especially near a pond, it can feel as if it is raining toads.

Toads and roads do not mix. In some places you may even see a 'toads crossing' sign. Thanks to Kenneth Grahame's Mr Toad, these creatures do not have a reputation for careful driving, but you can do them a favour by keeping an eye out.

26 MARCH | WHITE DEAD-NETTLE

White dead-nettles are much smarter and more statuesque than their scruffy red cousins.

Pick one – you are allowed – and look at it closely. A square stem encircled by a choir of white angel flowers with nettle-like leaves; it even has a less common woodland cousin called yellow archangel.

When I was a child I would try to steal some nectar from the bees. I would pull the whole bloom from the stem and suck gently on the slim neck of the flower. If I was lucky I got there before the first bee and would experience a tiny jet of sweetness.

27 MARCH | LAWN

As soon as the ground is dry enough, you should mark spring by lying down on a patch of grass and looking at the world from an inch above the ground.

Flies and bees will buzz above your head. You may see an ant or a spider. Blades of grass will sway in the breeze like a tall African savannah.

The best lawns are unfertilised and full of daisies, selfheal, catsear and even the occasional violet. In nature you can see them on the machair dunes of Scottish islands or high up on a mountain pasture.

If you are lucky enough to have a patch of lawn then that is your template. Unless you plan to play a game of bowls, please try to forbear the urge for perfection and ignore the adverts for fertiliser and weedkiller. Not much lives in bright green perfection. If it looks really neat, it's probably dead …

28 MARCH | TREE LISTENING

Stand close to a tree and listen.

You may hear young leaves above, or birds in the branches. What you cannot hear, though, is the sound of the giant tree engine throbbing into life.

Trees are giant pumps, sucking water through their roots and blasting it out into the air through their leaves, along with fresh gulps of oxygen for us all to breathe.

If you listen to them with a stethoscope at this time of year then you can hear them pumping – just like a beating heart. You might also hear the wheezing lungs of water-rich sapwood.

It is March and the sap is rising.

29 MARCH | HARTSTONGUE FERN

There are four types of fern that are common and easy to learn, so let's begin with the hartstongue. Ferns are the specialists of damp and shady places, inhabitants of a Victorian Gothic novel.

The Victorians were obsessed with ferns and the hartstongue was one of their favourites. Trainloads of ferns arrived in London from southwest England to satisfy the obsessive affliction of pteridomania – the fern craze of the late 19th century.

I think of ferns as looking like bracken (that's one for later in the year). But by that yardstick, this one doesn't look like a fern at all. It is named for its fancied resemblance to the tongue of a deer, and in April the long, pale green, undivided leaves unfurl from the late winter leaf mulch. The bright, glossy leaves catch dew and sunlight even on the darkest day.

The young leaves open with the characteristic fern-like spiral at the tip of the leaf and I think that is the easiest way to distinguish them from all the other emerging leaves at this time of year.

30 MARCH | ORCHARD

It is still not too late to plant a fruit tree. If you want some inspiration, then take a trip to an orchard, for if you want to plant a tree of any variety I would suggest that you start with an apple, pear or plum. You can pick one that will grow to any size you wish and choose the fruit that you like.

An orchard in March is dream-like, a haze of blossom above your head and long, damp grass around your feet: beautiful, rich in nature and a provider of food and ceremonies alike.

Orchards once formed part of every town and village and even the green corners of cities. Here you would find cider apples, pears, cherries or mazzards, plums and damsons. North Kent still has hazelnut orchards. In a decade we could make that true once again if we so chose – so this year mine is a dwarf Victoria plum, what's yours?

31 MARCH | GLOUCESTERSHIRE APPLE VARIETIES

Brandy · redstreak · dainty maids · crackstalk · Kenchy pippin · Lake's kernel · leathercoat · Lemon roy · Peggy red · Brown French · Ashmead's kernel · Ampney red · Arlingham churchyard · Lodgemore nonpareil · Longney russet · Netherton nonesuch · Hen's Turds · Holbert's Victoria · Flower of the west · Yellow Styre · Taynton codlin · Welsh druid · Red Dick · Pedington Brandy · Old Tankard · Nine of diamonds · Croome kernel · Rusty coat · Overton red

APRIL

April has always been marked for arrivals and rebirth. The days are edged with song: a chorus of new birds as the dawn appears and a sunset reprise of thrush and blackbird song from rooftops and trees.

Nestlings hatch and take wing. Each day a new insect appears on the flowers. Butterflies sketch yellow- and orange-tipped paths across the scene. Parks and lawns are candied with daisies and decked with dandelions.

It feels as though spring is rushing to delight. Each day there is something new to note and something not to miss.

Left: Orange-tip butterflies on garlic mustard.

1 APRIL | SOUTH WIND

'If ever I heard blessing it is there, where birds in trees that shoals and shadows are.' ('April Rise', Laurie Lee)

April is the time for arrivals. One or two of our summer migrants appear in March, but as soon as the wind turns south in April my ears prick up, listening for the summer birds. Willow warbler and chiffchaff are here – swallow, martin, cuckoo and swift yet to come.

In Greek mythology Notus, the south wind, is associated with searing summer heat. Here, it represents the arrival of spring, breathing warmth over the still-chilled ground and filling the air with buzzing insects.

2 APRIL | DAISY

This is the first flower any child should learn. The best lawns are speckled white with daisies.

These are the Norse god Freya's flower – symbol of love and fertility. They have a soft yellow centre and a ray of white, pink-tipped petals. The daisy family (Asteraceae) is one of the most widespread of all. It includes tree daisies, sunflowers and, my favourite, the Fjordland daisy from southern New Zealand, resident of the high wild mountains above Captain Cook's Doubtful Sound.

You can pick as many daisies as you like – they like nothing better than to be mown short. A new set of flowers will appear as if by magic within a day or two, and who wouldn't want to mark a spring day with a small posy of daisies?

3 APRIL | GARLIC MUSTARD

Jack-by-the-hedge is one of the definitive April flowers. It lives up to its name, favouring hedge banks, verges and shady spots. The plants can grow really tall and they have nettle-like leaves.

It lights up a spring lane with clusters of four-petalled flowers that give way to long, thin seeds, which are an important food for birds.

If you pick one and crush it you will get a distinct hit of garlic. I am told that you can use it in salads or even use it to make pesto.

4 APRIL | ORANGE TIP

This is the second true butterfly of spring. As soon as the temperatures rise, the male butterflies with their orange-tipped wings appear to patrol gardens and verges restlessly in search of a mate.

They favour the four-petalled flowers of the crucifer or mustard family, so if you want them to pause, then let the grass grow long enough for cuckoo flower and garlic mustard to thrive. Make your observation a swift one as they don't stay long – off searching for their more elusive partner. Female orange tips simply have black edges to their wings and tend to wait around on the sidelines rather than strut on the dancefloor.

Although they are easy to spot, it is said that 'once a bird has tasted an orange tip it is unlikely to repeat the experience.' (*The Butterflies of Britain and Ireland*, Jeremy Thomas and Richard Lewington, 1991.) If you spend your days living on mustardy plants, you probably do not make for a nice meal.

5 APRIL | SWALLOW

The hirundines – martins and swallows, along with their cousins, the swifts – are the companions of summer.

At this time of year, I am on tenterhooks, watching out for the first arrivals. Gilbert White suffered the same affliction when it came to this bird family. In a letter to the lawyer and naturalist Daines Barrington in January 1775 he wrote that the swallow '… is undoubtedly the first comer of all the British hirundines; and appears in general on or about the 13th of April, as I have remarked from many years observation.'

I think they now get here a touch earlier, and I have 5 April as 'swallow day' in my diary.

Swallows are metallic blue with long tail streamers and a dash of fire-red at their throat, and you will most likely see them first gliding low over the meadow grass or dipping into a pond.

6 APRIL | MAGNOLIA

The more that you watch nature, the more the passing of the seasons marks your life, to the extent that natural events merge with memories. So it is with magnolia for me.

Wherever the soil is sandy, you can grow a magnolia tree. You do this in hope of a few perfect days of white spring flowers: tulip-like *M. grandiflora*, or the stars of *M. stellata*.

It is an adopted tree here; most of the varieties you see in gardens come from China and Japan. It is mainly pollinated by beetles because, if you can believe this, it evolved before bees did. If the prospect of brief beauty is not sufficient then surely that is a reason to grow one.

7 APRIL | OAK FLOWER

Look closely at an oak tree. At this time of year oaks break into the softest green leaves. Dangling like a small chandelier beneath them are pale yellow-green flowers. Drop your inhibitions and give it a hug.

Oak is a truly wondrous tree. It supports hundreds of other specialist insects and fungi and an oak can live for a thousand years or more. Nearly all oak trees are hollow and they can survive for hundreds more years in that state.

Our oak trees are not only sources of building timber and firewood. They once provided bark for tanning leather, acorns for feeding pigs and oak apples for ink.

If an oak tree takes more than three of you to cuddle it then it is something really special – a tree that dates back to the English Civil War or even earlier, to the time of Elizabeth I.

8 APRIL | BROAD BUCKLER FERN

This is one of the big woodland ferns. Each huge frond is made up of dozens of mirror images – a great fractal mirage. The spiralling opening of a young fern leaf is one of the wonders of nature.

There are a few very similar ferns, but this is one of the most common. None of them are bracken, which we will meet later – because *bracken has branches.* Other ferns do not. Once you have learned that you will never mix the two up again.

Most ferns (bracken is the exception) love shade and humidity. They reproduce by spores, which need a damp environment. In the right conditions ferns can fill the scene: a fern-clad bank of a woodland stream is a thing of wonder. The Victorians (who seemed to have a fascination with shade) loved them.

9 APRIL | RED CAMPION

I am not strong on colours, but I am pretty sure that red campions are actually pink rather than red. They are a common plant of spring woodlands, adding a contrast to the bluebells, and also line road verges at this time of year.

Bees see colours differently as well, and a red campion is an example of a plant that is anything but plain when seen though their eyes.

When viewed through ultraviolet light (as bees do), you can see that red campion has a pattern that lures the insects in towards a central point.

In the slow, polite war that is plant evolution, some flowers use scent to attract insects. By contrast, campions are one of those flowers that instead use 'landing lights' to attract incoming flights.

10 APRIL | HOLLY BLUE

Here is a good reason to leave some ivy among the trees or on a sunny wall. Even in the heart of a city, you have a good chance of seeing a holly blue, frequenter of gardens and churchyards.

The reason is that ivy, together with holly, provides the main food plant for the caterpillars of the holly blue. For me, this is invariably the first blue butterfly of the year.

It is a silvery azure-blue, often seen flying high above you. If you can get close enough to see the closed wings you will see that the silver-blue is adorned by a delicate array of black spots.

11 APRIL | WILLOW WARBLER

Try setting a birdsong as your ringtone. This month it has to be willow warbler: a rapid descending trill that, according to Edward Grey, Viscount of Fallodon, was 'soft as summer rain'. (*The Charm of Birds*, 1927.)

It can be really hard to tune in to the songs of birds, but if you can get to know the song of a willow warbler then it is a delight to hear the first of the year – usually, for me, on an early April day.

They are close cousins of the chiffchaff, whose call I hope you heard in March. You probably won't see one – they are another pale brownish, skulking type. Each year a huge wave of willow warblers floods in from Europe, filling woods and parks with their song.

The flaw in this ringtone plan, of course, will arise if you happen to receive an urgent call while surrounded by a spring chorus of willow warblers. I suggest that this is a risk worth taking.

12 APRIL | EASTER BUNNY

Young rabbits are out and about already and you may see one to mark your Easter Day.

It turns out that the whole idea of an 'Easter bunny' is in fact an import from Germany. Equally the rabbit itself is a relatively recent arrival. It had been thought that the Normans brought them here for food and fur. However, it turns out, from recent analysis of a bone originally found in 1964 at Fishbourne Palace in Chichester, West Sussex, that the Romans kept them as pets.

I also have a soft spot for the rabbits that have made their home here. They are having a tough time of it with disease, but where they

do thrive they are little nature engineers. Around their warrens, they create a quite distinctive 'rabbit lawn' landscape of short turf and bare ground that is insect-filled and flower-rich.

13 APRIL | GERMANDER SPEEDWELL

The speedwell is the traveller's companion – plant of roads and waysides. You may not wish to follow the Irish tradition of stitching it into your coat for luck, but you should take a moment to stop and take a closer look.

Speedwells flower nearly all year round, but April is time for the germander speedwell, with soft, mint-like leaves and bright blue cat's-eye flowers with two little horned anthers.

The flowers are tiny but intricately beautiful and they go by a host of folk names: gypsyweed, eye of the child Jesus, bird's eye, cat's eye, farewell. They wish you good speed as you pass by.

14 APRIL | AQUILEGIA

April is the time for woodland flowers. Many of them flower and set seed before the leaves of trees cast a deep shade.

Aquilegia is one of these, a scarce and scattered wild plant of limestone woods. You will be lucky to find it, a brief flowering wonder by a stony path, but it is also a wonderful plant to grow in gardens.

The blue flowers are said to look like five doves clustered together, which gives rise to the common name of columbine – from the Latin *colomba*, meaning dove.

I favour the Latin name of *Aquilegia*, derived from the Latin *aquila*, which refers to the eagle-talon shape of the tops of the flowers. Either way it is an April delight.

15 APRIL | HOUSE MARTIN

Who wouldn't love these birds that choose to live alongside us?

Soon after the swallows appear the house martins arrive as well. They come to construct temporary mud dwellings under the eaves of houses.

If the swallow was a car, then it would be some kind of exotic sports car. A house martin, by contrast, is more of a reliable runabout. The more you watch them the easier they are to tell apart.

If you get a good view, house martins are easy to distinguish with their white rear and short V-notch of a tail. Swallows, conversely, have a long tail and a blue back.

I never cease to marvel at the fact that this tiny migrant has flown here all the way from southern Africa to raise a family just next door.

16 APRIL | COLLARED DOVE

These are doves, rather than pigeons, sporting a smart, black shirt collar on an almost blush-pink set of feathers.

You may see one beneath your bird feeder. This is all part of a secret plan on the part of collared doves to take over the world. In the past century, they have spread out from their original home in the tropics to most of the Northern Hemisphere. They are the new kids on the block – they didn't breed in this country until the 1950s.

They carry themselves as if they are a cut above our humble wood pigeon and as a result I don't feel quite as fond of them. They also sing a little like a broken squeaky toy.

17 APRIL | RED MASON BEE

Not all bees are sociable and not all of them sting. Red mason bees are one example and they are out and about in April. They are more ginger than red and they are absolutely fantastic pollinators – used by commercial fruit growers to increase their yields.

Red mason bees like to nest in soft brickwork, so in April you may see them scouting out old nail holes in south-facing walls.

If you like you can give them a helping hand by making a bee hotel; a few hollow stems packed together make a perfect place for a female mason bee to make a nest. You will know when she has done so when you see a stem packed with mud.

18 APRIL | WOOD ANEMONE

Spring is a time to go out into the woods.

Some of our woods have been recorded on maps since the early seventeenth century, and in the vast majority of cases we can be confident that they were woodland long before that, sometimes dating back to the last Ice Age.

These are called 'ancient' woods and they are really special. If you can find one then you may also find the windflower, the wood anemone.

In some places it can carpet the ground with fine dissected foliage and perfect white flowers with seven or eight 'petals' (actually sepals).

It is another plant that you see high up in the European mountains, but here it has become stuck in the woods as it rarely sets seed, spreading at most by 6ft (1.8m) every hundred years through its roots alone.

19 APRIL | HEDGE

Hedges are tiny linear patches of woodland that knit our landscape together. They often mark subtle changes in soil type or moisture between fields, or they may follow the line of a ditch or parish boundary. They are anything but random.

My favourite hedges are tall and thick with hedgerow trees poking out of the top, not those sorrowful, neat 4ft (1.2m) high affairs with gaps between their legs. That said, a freshly laid hedge, with branches bent diagonally and neat stakes and binders to hold them tight, is also a thing of great beauty.

Many of our hedges date from the enclosure of the landscape in the eighteenth century and these are often dominated by hawthorn. In other parts of the country hedges may be much older. There is a lovely rule of thumb called Hooper's rule that helps you date an old hedge. Simply count the number of different types of woody shrubs on a 30-pace length and multiply by 110 years.

20 APRIL | ASPEN

'All day and night, save winter, every weather,
Above the inn, the smithy, and the shop,
The aspens at the cross-roads talk together
Of rain, until their last leaves fall from the top.'
('Aspens', Edward Thomas, 1915.)

Listen out for an aspen.

There are not many plants that you can hear before you see them. Reeds perhaps, gorse on a hot day, but none compare with the tremulous-leaved aspen.

The aspen is never still. The flattened stems that bear the diamond-shaped leaves are always whispering.

This is one of the poplar family, fast-growing and light-timbered, with grey bark that is often marked with black diamonds. It crops up in groups along rivers and in damp places. And it's a tree that talks!

21 APRIL | NETTLE

Nettles are fierce in April.

I don't need to describe them further as they are one of the first plants anyone learns. Nettle stings on your wrists and bramble scratches on your ankles – the stigmata of the amateur naturalist.

They are a sign of fertile soil and often turn up in places enriched by human habitation. The young leaf tips are edible, and in the past nettles were widely eaten by those who struggled to put food on the table. These days, however, they appear on many restaurant menus and in wild food recipes.

They are hard plants to love, but do leave some if you can. The caterpillars of four of our most beautiful butterflies depend largely on nettles – red admiral, small tortoiseshell, peacock and comma. Just like some spiky people, this plant can be the source of the most unexpected joy.

22 APRIL | DOCK

If you have just been stung by a nettle, then you will quickly need to find a dock leaf – large, stout leaves as big as your foot.

Find a dock and rub it on the sting until your skin turns lizard green. It seems to work, but perhaps mainly because distraction is the best antidote to pain.

It's a wonderful thing to teach to children. It gives them a way to help each other when one of them gets hurt and they are really good at recognising the right type of leaf.

Happily, nettle and dock often grow together as they are both lovers of deep, nitrogen-rich soil: poison and antidote, side by side.

23 APRIL | HERB ROBERT

This is the plant that grows in the gaps between pavement and fence, or indeed anywhere. Shallow-rooted herb robert turns up in hedges, fields and even along coastal shores.

It straggles with hairy, purplish stems that curl upwards from a central core. If it is dry the leaves turn red as well. It has five-petalled, five pence piece-sized pink flowers that rapidly turn into beak-shaped seedheads that identify it as being part of the geranium or cranesbill family.

Herb robert is supposed to ease toothache and nosebleeds and repel mosquitoes if rubbed on the skin. The smell may take a bit of getting used to – it is also known as 'stinking Bob' and has a mouse-like aroma!

For me its ability to enliven a pavement crack is an even greater benefit.

24 APRIL | GREENFINCH

Unlike their thriving cousins the goldfinch, greenfinches are in decline – but they are still common enough for you to see on the bird feeder if you are lucky.

Their large bill is good for cracking seeds, which means that they can eat things that other finches cannot. While a goldfinch may be the master at extracting teasel seeds, a greenfinch can deal with tougher fare – yew berries and rosehip seeds.

You might hear them as they fly by; their call is a bit of an odd, wheezy note, like a gate that needs oiling.

In spring the bright green males show off with extravagant, looping song flights, showing off in search of a mate, flashing the bright yellow stripe on their wings.

The rest of the year they seem more shy, as if they dislike being watched, so if you see one, be sure to pretend you are looking at something else or they are inclined to fly off.

25 APRIL | ST MARK'S FLY

Today is the feast of St Mark, something much celebrated in the Eastern Orthodox Church, but less so in the UK.

Nonetheless, today is the day to see the St Mark's Fly.

It's a great big, dozy black fly, it looks a bit like a house fly and if you go to any damp place you may see this shiny black character with dangling legs mooching about. They quite often land on you for a rest, but don't worry, they don't bite.

What is the point of flies, you may ask? Their larvae are part of the cycle that decomposes dead material. These flies are great pollinators of fruit trees. An emergence of flies in April is also perfect timing for all the birds who are trying to feed their young.

So don't swat it, notice it. Incredibly, it is one of 7,000 different types of fly to which our small islands play host, and we are finding more varieties every year.

26 APRIL | WHITETHROAT

Here is another bird for your spring song collection. It is really quite common, but you could reasonably have never heard of it. You have now had a fortnight to perfect the willow warbler ringtone – so this is the advanced class.

The whitethroat is another bird that shouts 'spring' and arrives in the middle of April. It has quite a distinctive song, which once learned means that whitethroats magically go from 'never heard of it' to 'hear them all the time'.

I can do no better than this description from a classic bird book in my bookcase – *Let's Watch the Birds* by W. Percival Westell (1943) – 'The Greater Whitethroat has an ash-grey head, the feathers of which are raised perceptibly as the male utters its scratchy impetuous song, its white throat swelling as it does so.'

27 APRIL | KINGCUP

In the right places, the riverbanks are decked with glorious giant yellow flowers, but you might need to get your feet wet to have a closer look.

These are the marsh marigold or kingcups. They look like buttercups that have had a growth spurt, with large round leaves and huge yellow flowers.

In Ireland the Gaelic name for kingcup is the flower of Beltane, the pagan Mayday festival; it was one of the flowers brought into houses to mark the season.

I love the array of names that people have given them: brave bassinets, bull flower, cow lily, crazy Beth, crowfoot, drunkards, goldes, gools, horse blob, May blob, mare blob, marybuds, meadow-bright, meadow gowan, publican's cloak, publicans-and-sinners, soldier's buttons, water boots, water dragon, water gowan, yellow gowan.

28 APRIL

BLUEBELL

'There is a silent eloquence in every wild bluebell that fills my softened heart with bliss.' (From 'The Bluebell', Anne Brontë, 1840.)

If you possibly can, get outside now and soften your heart with one of the wonders of these islands – a bluebell wood. Other countries have bluebells, but very few can produce a carpet of woodland bluebells to rival those of the UK.

The Brontë sisters treasured them and they are beloved of writers and poets. In a nice bit of symmetry, the juice from crushed bluebell bulbs once provided the glue for binding books.

But they are not just a woodland flower, they also carpet some of the sea islands of west Wales and the Hebrides. Catching sight of a puffin emerging from a mass of bluebells has to count as one of my stranger nature experiences.

29 APRIL | CUCKOO

Today is my day to hope for the song of a cuckoo. It is my eldest son's birthday and it is also cuckoo day. Sometimes it comes a little earlier and sometimes slightly later, but around about now my ears are pricked listening for a distant cuckoo call.

Male cuckoos often sing as they fly in, and if you are lucky enough to see one, they look almost like a hawk, with a looping flight and long tail.

But the song is the thing. They are rare now, so your best chance is to listen out near scrubby land and reed-beds. The time to hear them sing is from now until early June, while they are pairing with females who go on to lay eggs stealthily in the nests of other birds, to be raised by foster parents.

Until recently we knew little about them, but we now know that many of our cuckoos spend their winter in the Congo. The adults head back as early as July, leaving their children to navigate alone to their winter quarters, guided only by instinct and the Earth's magnetic field.

30 APRIL | COMMON POND DWELLERS

Common toad · great crested newt · grass snake · club-tailed dragonfly · crayfish · depressed river mussel · fairy shrimp · freshwater pearl mussel · glutinous snail · medicinal leech · pond mud snails · pondweed leafhopper · striped mayfly · tadpole shrimp · common frog · smooth newt · palmate newt · alderflies · caddisflies · damselflies · dragonflies · mayflies · pond skaters · shrimps · water beetles · water boatmen · water slaters

MAY

The hazel leaves start to hang heavy and sag the boughs. Fulsome May blossom lights overgrown corners. Cow parsley foams the verge.

The grass grows by the minute. Swifts cruise in and mayflies dance. The setting sun marches northwards each night, and it's the time to stay outside until it is quite dark, waiting until the robins quieten, hoping for the flit of a bat in the twilight.

Left: Cow parsley.

1 MAY | MAY DAY

'The trees are coming into leaf. Like something almost being said …' (From 'The Trees', Philip Larkin, 1967.)

The hawthorn blossom will not peak for a week or two yet, but today you should cut a stem or two for the house. Traditionally you can do so on May Day without fear of bad luck.

May Day is the height of spring in the Northern Hemisphere and in every culture it seems to be an excuse for a party. The Romans had a flower festival for the goddess Flora – which seemed mainly to involve flowers and nakedness. The pagans celebrate Beltane with fires and greenwood marriages. Christians in Northern Europe and Scandinavia celebrate Walpurgis night on the eve of May Day with bonfires, singing, dancing and playing pranks.

Whatever your preference, today you have an excuse to fill your house with flowers, light the last fire of winter and take part in a bit of dancing.

'Last year is dead … begin afresh, afresh, afresh.'

2 MAY | POLLINATION

A small act of kindness is to help our insects at this time of year by letting the grass grow longer and the flowers appear.

It is actually a small act of self-interest. Bees and other insects provide the free service of pollinating most of the crops on which we depend, and they need a bit of help in return.

Plants have developed all sorts of tricks to entice insects, moths and even bats to help them reproduce. Bright colours (sometimes only visible to insects) and the promise of sweet nectar lure them in, the pollen sticks to the creature in question and is taken on to the next flower where it fertilises the egg cells to make seeds.

If you watch closely you will see honey bees harvesting pollen to carry it back to their hives in pollen baskets on their hind legs. I prefer watching the less subtle approach of a bumble bee as it dives into a flower and emerges showered in pollen as if it has just been flour-bombed.

So put the lawn mower away for a spell, let the grass grow long and sit and watch the pollinators at work instead.

3 MAY | DAWN CHORUS

Today is a good time to get up before dawn and go outside. The early bird catches the worm, and the early human can catch the dawn chorus – for the beginning of May is dawn chorus season.

It starts as soon as there is a hint of light – perhaps an hour before the sun rises. Our friends the blackbird, thrush and robin are usually among the first.

It is thought that dawn is a good time to attract a mate and mark out a territory. There is not much food about this early in the year, so it's a time for showing off instead, and for birds the quality of your singing voice makes a difference to your success.

All of that effort deserves a little appreciation – and you will be home in time to go back to bed for an hour if you are lucky.

4 MAY | SPECKLED WOOD BUTTERFLY

This is the first woodland butterfly of spring, dancing in and out of shafts of light in between the trees, skirmishing in shrubby alleyways or resting on a bramble leaf.

They are chocolate and cream, with a faint chequered pattern and tiny black 'eyes' on each wing, and it is worth being patient to get a closer look. You can't mistake them for anything else, which makes a pleasant change for the nature watcher.

Later in the year they will be laying single green eggs on blades of grass, but in spring they seem mostly to spin upwards in pairs, soaking up the May sun.

5 MAY | BRAMBLE

Whenever someone says the word 'bramble', it is invariably preceded by a phrase like 'get rid of'. That speaks of their success, perhaps. There are over 300 species of bramble, and there is even a name for someone who studies them – a batologist.

The reason we have brambles is because these islands were once filled with huge browsing animals. Just beyond the horizon of recorded history is the memory of huge cattle such as aurochs and bison, wild horses, boar and elk-like deer. In a landscape like this, thorns offer a serious competitive advantage. Bramble thickets still play that role today: protecting young trees from grazing, but not casting such a dense shade that they cannot grow in the first place.

Bramble plants are an incredibly valuable source of nectar for butterflies and other insects. Later in the year they also provide blackberries for people and birds alike.

They are a real pain in a flower bed, but I feel that there should always be a few places where we might learn to live alongside them.

6 MAY | BUTTERCUP

Hold a buttercup under someone's chin to see if they like butter. If it shines yellow, they do. After all, who doesn't really like butter? More to the point, who wouldn't want someone to hold a buttercup under their chin?

Buttercups are very shiny flowers and the pollen does stain your chin. They are also not very palatable to animals, so over time a wet meadow can fill with buttercups.

We don't appreciate a buttercup meadow as much as we should. They scream 'May' in vibrant yellow. In some places the buttercups pick out the furrows of the old shared fields from medieval times, filling them with gold.

7 MAY | RIBWORT PLANTAIN

This is another plant of childhood – it grows alongside pavements. You may not know it by name, but you will know it by sight.

It has a flat rosette of lance-like leaves and a single, long wiry stem with an oval flower head that sports a white fascinator of flowers.

Ribwort plantain seems to like growing in trodden-down places, but it was once an important medicinal plant.

We used them to play a game we called 'conkers'. Pick a long stem and whip it against your opponent's stem. The first to behead the opposition is the winner. Once you get bored with that, you can pick another to make a missile by looping the stem on itself and firing the head at a friend.

8 MAY | HEDGEHOG

'Hedgehogs abound in my gardens and fields' wrote the Reverend Gilbert White in Hampshire in 1789. Happily we still have them now, albeit in smaller numbers.

They are brilliant little animals that live alongside us, covered in spines, and with the neat trick of rolling into a ball when threatened. I know that I have hedgehogs in my garden because they once woke me up while mating (saying whatever amounts to 'Ouch' in hedgehog language, I presume).

Gardens are really important for these strange little animals. About this time of year they may already have given birth to young, so it's a good time to look out for them, and perhaps give them a helping hand.

9 MAY | COW PARSLEY

The verges of early May are suddenly head high with a foam of cow parsley: cream saucers of flowers that buzz with insects.

There are lots of plants that look like cow parsley, but there is only one that takes over the whole scene for a fortnight in May, sometimes early in May and sometimes later, depending on the spring.

It is beautiful and transient – by early June it has given way to other things.

For me, these will always be the flowers for my wedding day. Call me a cheapskate, but I thought that tubs of cow parsley lining the aisle looked rather fabulous. It also means that nature can help to remind me my wedding anniversary is approaching …

10 MAY | MAYFLY

Sit by a river on a warm afternoon in early May and you may just see the dance of the mayflies.

The adults emerge to mate and live only for a single day. Yet the species has been around so long that they pre-date the dinosaurs. They are also a good measure of a clean river.

These remarkable insects spend most of their life (up to two years) underwater. They are the flies much imitated by trout and salmon fishermen and, despite the name, you may see one of the 50 or so varieties at any point during the summer.

They are unmistakable, with large wings, a long body held upright and a three-stranded aerial of a tail. On a muggy day in May you will see clouds of them dancing upwards and descending, repeating one of the very oldest natural rituals on Earth.

11 MAY | FORGET-ME-NOT

In between writing *The Rime of the Ancient Mariner* (please don't make me read it again) and the opium-inspired *Kubla Khan* (I am a big fan), Samuel Taylor Coleridge found time to popularise the flower name 'forget-me-not' from a German folk tale.

The source of the name can be traced to the poem 'The Keepsake', which was published in 1802.

Prior to that, this beautiful little spring flower had been known as mouse's ear or scorpion grass after its curling flower stems.

The flowers are a sweet pale blue with a yellow eye. They are brilliantly adaptable plants; different varieties are found in waste ground and fields, along streams and in woodland.

The most common variety also neatly fills gaps in flower beds.

12 MAY | BLACK MEDICK

I have a soft spot for any plant that grows beside pavements. The black medick has a fondness for compacted soil, so a nice tyre track or well-trodden shortcut suits it fine.

It is a humble weed with a small, yellow, clover-like flower and leaves that comprise three leaflets. Like the other trefoils (clovers) this is one of the food plants for common blue caterpillars.

It's a useful plant for humans as it fixes nitrogen into the soil, and for that reason it has followed humans around the world. Medick does not refer to medical properties – instead it comes from the Greek name for the plant, suggesting it is originally from Media, now north-western Iran.

13 MAY | CLOUDS

We now understand that the air, the plants and our soil and rocks are connected. The notion that the things that we are made of – oxygen, nitrogen, carbon and sulphur – are part of a great flow between air, living things, sea and rock is one of the most mind-boggling ideas.

The easiest to understand is the water cycle – an example of something we learned at school and then never thought about again, like oxbow lakes and calculus.

Look at the clouds and reflect on the fact that part of the ocean has taken up temporary residence over your head. I am firmly of the view that feeling small is good for you, and ten minutes looking at clouds is seriously restorative.

They also have some great names. I think my favourite is 'mackerel sky' – which reminds us not just of the ocean, but also of the pattern on the shimmering fish within it that illuminates a fine May evening.

14 MAY | HAWTHORN BLOSSOM

'Rough winds do shake the darling buds of May; and summer's lease hath all too short a date.' (From Sonnet 18, William Shakespeare, 1609.)

The May blossom in the sonnet adorns our humble hawthorn bush. For this brief fortnight it lights every uncut stem with a spray of white flowers.

In a moment the landscape is bathed in flowers; verges light up and waste ground becomes beautiful. May blossom is everywhere.

Stop the clock please. Part of me wishes it could always be mid-May in its brief perfection.

Yet as the sonnet hints, the perfection and the passing are part of the same thing. It is May and the whole summer lies ahead. The seasons turn, yet for the hawthorn, 'thy eternal summer shall not fade'.

15 MAY | COWSLIP

These flowers look like a host of tiny primroses on stalks and can fill whole fields with creamy yellow.

They are a sign of good, flower-rich grassland. They have leaves just like a primrose and are one of the defining flowers of May.

They have all sorts of common names: freckled face, golden drops, bunch of keys, fairies' flower, lady's fingers, long legs and milk maidens.

They are also the food plant for one of our rarest butterflies, the wonderfully named Duke of Burgundy, but that is the subject of other nature books.

16 MAY | HORSE CHESTNUT FLOWER

Oak tree flowers may be modest, but those of the conker tree are most definitely not.

Horse chestnut or conker flowers pepper the exterior of the dark-leaved trees as if it has been dressed with candles for Christmas. Close up the flowers are the size of an upside-down knickerbocker glory, cream and pink with dots of yellow.

Conkers are the tree equivalent of chicken tikka masala, a tree of the Balkan mountains so comprehensively adopted by the British that it's hard to imagine that they have only been here for a couple of centuries.

But, of course, when you look closely at them it is obvious that they hail from a foothill somewhere out towards the East. As well as their exotic flowers, they have huge, five-fingered leaves as big as your hand, thick bark and a seed (our humble conker) that wouldn't look out of place washed up on the beach of a desert island.

17 MAY | BURDOCK LEAF

Outside my house there grows a wild plant with huge leaves. The seedheads, about the size of a boiled sweet, are covered in tiny hooks. My children used to delight in hurling them at me.

This is the sticky bomb plant. The seeds stick to your clothes and make you itch. For now, the huge leaves are all you can see and they are elephant-like, hard to mistake for anything else. Later the young sticky bombs will emerge dressed in purple flowers.

This is an amazing plant. You can make dandelion and burdock drink from the roots, and the seeds inspired the creator of Velcro.

18 MAY | PEACOCK

This is the most wondrous of butterflies: deep red with four huge, bright eyes. Peacocks love a garden or a park and are one of those butterflies that settles obligingly to let you take a closer look.

When perched on a flower you can miss them entirely, as with their wings closed they are almost black, like a dead leaf. If frightened they resort to scare tactics and reveal the eyes of a huge creature by opening their wings.

Unlike some other butterflies they hibernate over winter in dark, cosy places, cracks in trees, roof spaces and sheds, so you may see one even earlier in the year if you wake it from its slumber.

19 MAY | CINNABAR MOTH

Any time from now you may find some yellow and black caterpillars clustered on the flowers of yellow ragwort.

These exotic fellows are the young of the cinnabar moth – a vibrant red and black moth, which loves scruffy grassland.

It's one of a number of moths that likes to be out and about during the daytime and it is named for the bright red mineral from which mercury is extracted.

If you are happy to provide a daily supply of ragwort you could even try bringing up a caterpillar at home; there are few natural things as amazing as the transmutation from caterpillar to moth or butterfly.

20 MAY | ROWAN FLOWER

This is a plant with eagle-feather leaves, blood-red berries and flowers like ambrosia. In Greek mythology, the goddess Hebe had the task of feeding cups of life-giving ambrosia to the Gods. When the cup fell into the hands of demons, an eagle was sent to fetch it back, and when blood and feathers flew in the ensuing fight, each drop that fell back to Earth became a rowan tree.

These medium-sized trees really look most at home next to a fast-running stream and the rowan has a long association with magical powers.

Yet they are common in streets, gardens and churchyards, with soft, ash-like leaves and grey bark. At this time of year they are decked with foamy white flowers filled with insects in search of their own dose of life-giving ambrosia.

21 MAY | BEATING THE BOUNDS

Ascension Day (the fortieth day after Easter) marks the date of the old tradition of 'beating the bounds' – an annual walk around the parish boundary that dates right back to Saxon times, if not before.

A regular circuit is a great way of noticing things. As you do this, the plants and trees will become familiar friends: the oak tree on the corner; the bramble with the tastiest blackberries from last year; the place where the sparrows chatter or the heron hunts.

Where you go determines what you see. The trees and shrubs are fixed by their roots. Most of the plants grow in the same place each year. Likewise, many of the insects have very specific tastes in plants, so their occurrence is often predictable. Once they have nested, lots of birds remain in the same place – it is not just a song thrush on top of that tree, it is probably the same song thrush you have seen there before.

This sounds like a parochial exercise, but it is anything but. While you are walking your little local circuit, you might want to reflect on the parish boundary circumscribed by some of the plants and creatures that you see – from a wood anemone that spreads by a couple of feet every century, to a bird or two from Africa and a host of insects that have travelled here all the way from the Far East.

22 MAY | SKYLARK

May is a great time to find a singing skylark.

Skylarks are brownish birds with not much to distinguish them, but their song is simply beautiful. I don't think that any piece of music captures the spirit of a bird as perfectly as Vaughan Williams's 'A Lark Ascending'.

Larks soar from the ground and float upwards on helicopter wings singing a burbling, watery song all the while. Sometimes they go so high that one can barely see them, but the song carries nonetheless.

They once nested as a matter of course in fields of crops, but modern chemical agriculture is not their friend, so you will need an expanse of wild grassland or a field left fallow in order to find one.

23 MAY | SWIFT

Fix your eyes on the sky for the last of our avian summer guests.

By now you may have got to know the habits of house martins and swallows, circling above you, hunting for insects. Now they may be joined by swifts, scything through the spring sunset, jet black and lightning fast, swept back and sleek.

These are not earthly creatures, they are mystical dwellers of the air. We now know that they may only touch the ground when they return here for a brief couple of months to breed in colonies, usually in our oldest buildings.

They catch insects on the wing, they mate in the air and at night it is thought that they spiral upwards for a gliding catnap 3 miles (4.8km) above our heads.

24 MAY | BLACK APHID

You may notice an infestation of aphids – whole stems covered in tiny black insects, sucking the sap from the plant and sometimes even causing the leaves to curl.

You have a choice about how to think about this. The first option is to think in the way we humans like to think, which is to describe this as a pest problem and appoint ourselves as the people who need to solve it with some kind of chemical spray.

I would encourage you to choose an alternative. This is not an infestation, it is a feast. It is the insect equivalent of a herd of antelope at a watering hole. Try to resist the urge to get involved just yet. Watch and wait.

You may well see ants coming to feed off the honeydew, or a spiny ladybird larva with a meal in mind. Wait long enough and you will certainly get the larvae of hoverfly or fine lacewings. Blue tits will definitely join in too.

Nine times out of ten, if you can wait for three days, nature will solve the problem for you and be grateful for it.

If it is your favourite rose then you are allowed an exception – get out the soapy water and give the aphids a squirt.

25 MAY | DANISH SCURVY GRASS

This is the plant to spot in the central reservation of a dual carriageway, lining your route with white flowers atop fleshy green leaves.

Despite the name, it is one of our native plants. It is a plant of shingle banks and rocky shores, but recently it has crept inland at a dramatic pace. It's a reminder of the adaptability of plants. The application of salt to roads in winter creates conditions on the verges that are very similar to a sea spray-drenched shore.

As the name suggests, it is rich in vitamin C and was once eaten by sailors for that reason, which I suppose would only now come in handy in the event that you were suffering from scurvy and couldn't find a motorway services.

26 MAY

KESTREL

The kestrel above is sketching the shape of the wind, hanging against the flow of the breeze, '… as a skate's heel sweeps smooth on a bow-bend: the hurl and gliding, rebuffed the big wind.' (From 'The Windhover', Gerard Manley Hopkins, 1877.)

Gerard Manley Hopkins defined a new poetic form – sprung rhythm – as if words alone would not suffice to describe a kestrel. It is a hard poem to understand, but the words carry more than just meaning – when read they convey that air is a fluid, full of patterns and waves made visual by the instincts of this little falcon.

When there is less breeze the kestrel hovers, crucifix-like, and this makes them an easy bird to recognise.

Watch out for the hovering bird – it can only be a kestrel – gyroscope-still, spinning in a moment.

27 MAY | VERGE

Road verges are little strips of wilderness. At the beginning of May, some of them were yellow with cowslips. Now, the cow parsley is just fading, but it will give way to blue meadow cranesbill and hogweed soon enough.

Some road verges contain remnants of the woodlands they were once adjacent to, including wood anemone, bluebell and wild garlic On poorer soils, road verges can be full of rare and special plants. I can think of roundabouts full of wild orchids and a whole motorway flanked with wild daffodil.

28 MAY | YELLOW FLAG IRIS

Irises look too exotic to be native to this country. They seem to have crept from the gallery wall out of a French Impressionist painting.

In May, our streams and marshes are adorned with stunning yellow flags. They love having their feet in water and can form deep margins around ponds and lakes, with huge, grey-green, sword-shaped leaves and vivid yellow flowers. You could go and paint some yourself.

29 MAY | YELLOWHAMMER

This is the bird of open summer fields. It can sometimes appear almost completely bright yellow in flight. You will see it perched on a hedgerow or a wire: a walker's companion.

A yellowhammer nest is a thing of wonder. The eggs have a unique pattern, described by the poet John Clare as 'pen-scribbled o'er with ink their shells, resembling writing scrawls which fancy reads'. He knew them as the scribble lark.

The yellowhammer's song is a bit of a scribble too. They sing 'a little bit of bread and no cheese' – a monotone of notes with a flat refrain – which some credit as an inspiration for Beethoven's 5th. Personally I think it's a bit better than that …

30 MAY | INSECT FAMILIES

Alderflies · ants · antlions · Archaeognatha · barklice · bees · beetles · biting lice · booklice · butterflies · bugs · caddisflies · cockroaches · crickets · damselflies · dobsonflies · dragonflies · earwigs · fleas · flies · grasshoppers · lacewings · leaf insects · lice · mantids · mayflies · moths · praying mantids · scorpionflies · snakeflies · stick insects · stoneflies · strepsipterans · sucking lice · termites · three-pronged bristletails · thrips · true bugs · wasps · web-spinners · zorapterans · proturans · springtails · two-pronged bristletails

31 MAY | EGGSHELL

There is something bright in the dark green shade of the path. A pale blue half-domed egg: weightless, pebble-smooth. Stand still for a moment and look around. Nearby there will be an empty nest. There may also be a parent leading a phalanx of fluffy fledglings on a roving lesson about where to find food.

Once collecting eggs was a childhood pastime – which perhaps says less about social norms than about how many birds there once were in our landscape. Our birds are having a tough enough time without humans ganging up on them. But taking home an eggshell is something to be encouraged – an adornment for a summer windowsill.

JUNE

'June 3, 1769. Saw the planet Venus enter the disc of the sun. Just as the sun was setting the spot was very visible to the naked eye.'

The Reverend Gilbert White was at home in Selborne, Hampshire. Captain James Cook and Joseph Banks were watching the same sight from the island of Tahiti, trying to unravel the mysteries of longitude. There is more than one type of discovery and observation.

In June the year turns again around the solstice and nature takes a little pause for breath. Feel the grass under your bare feet. Contemplate an eternal evening and indulge in a little midsummer madness.

Left: Wild foxgloves.

1 JUNE | DANDELION CLOCK

Tell the time with a dandelion clock. Pick it, blow on it and watch. I find it's helpful to know roughly what the time is before I start to blow. But perhaps that's cheating.

Dandelion clocks are quite staggering bits of natural engineering; a perfect, moon-like arrangement of the finest seeds. They are much loved by artists and photographers.

Shakespeare knew them by their local name of chimney sweepers, 'Golden lads and girls all must, as chimney sweepers come to dust.' (From *Cymbeline*, 1623.) I can see the resemblance to an old chimney brush.

2 JUNE | SEED STRATEGIES

Look closely at a dandelion clock and you will see that each seed is attached to a tiny little parachute that is only released from the plant when the breeze is strong enough. Thistles have copied the same trick.

Other plants (such as the burdock – our sticky-bomb plant) would rather attach their seeds to a passing animal and use them as a transport service. Some tempt an animal to eat their seed and carry it in their guts to their destination, like mistletoe. Even better, how about encouraging a mildly forgetful animal to collect seed and bury it for a rainy day, like mice do with hazelnuts.

Alder seeds float, Himalayan balsam fires seeds like a cannon, sycamore seeds spin, orchids collaborate with fungi. Every plant has a strategy to give its offspring the best chance of getting to the right place in time for the right opportunity.

3 JUNE | CLEAVERS

Remember that annoying kid from school? There was a plant that they could not resist sticking on your back when you weren't looking. It has lots of nicknames: goosegrass, sticky bobs, kisses. We call it sticky weed.

It's a square-stemmed plant, covered in tiny hooks and little bobble seeds. It scrambles up the hedgerows and through flower beds so vigorously in June that it seems as if it is going to cover everything.

This is one of the bedstraw plants – once used as stuffing for mattresses. I think it would work much better than the finer yellow lady's bedstraw that is also in flower around now. It's a herbal remedy too – the leaves and stems can be cooked to make a tonic that cleans out toxins and the pulp can relieve bites, burns and stings.

Grab a handful from the hedge and take a closer look. Now, admit it, it is really tempting to stick it on to someone …

4 JUNE | ELDERFLOWER

Bury your nose in the smell of June: sweet, overpowering, lemony elderflower.

Even better, hunt out some young elderflowers and make some cordial. Give them a shake to free them of insects and then a long soak in some water for good measure.

It is a plant of paradoxes. Elder trees are scruffy, ragged things, but their flowers are a thing of wonder. In many cultures elder is regarded as a magical plant, yet it grows in the humblest of places.

5 JUNE | DOGWOOD

While hunting for elderflowers you may well come across another white flower – this time with clusters of four-pointed petals.

This is the dogwood, one of my favourite hedgerow shrubs. It forms a great spreading thicket of dense twigs and leaves – and if you cut it back it throws out even more straight stems.

The leaves have veins which curve along the edge of the leaf and for that reason our family call it the pizza plant. If you pull a leaf gently in half, it holds together with threads just like a pizza slice when you cut it.

The stems are deep red in winter and look attractive as a decoration. It is also (after hazel) my top choice for using as a marshmallow stick.

6 JUNE | FOXGLOVE

There is nothing nicer than spending a few minutes watching a bumble bee trying to reverse out of a foxglove.

Foxgloves are great tall spikes of flowers that favour disturbed woodland edges.

They are really exotic in appearance and their strategy is to lure bees into their long flowers and cover them in pollen to be transported to the next plant. It is not very subtle, but it is highly effective.

Despite the fact that I now know the plant is poisonous I still find it quite hard to resist putting foxglove flowers on my fingertips.

7 JUNE | WILD CABBAGE (RAPESEED)

Oilseed rape turns whole parts of the landscape yellow in early June. The plant also turns up anywhere the ground is disturbed – making huge plants with crucifix yellow flowers.

It's a very close relative of the wild cabbage, although that is now a rare plant, found only on a few sea cliffs.

Although big fields of oilseed rape are a relatively recent thing, the brassica family (turnips and cabbages) has long been incredibly useful in agriculture; the plants fix nitrogen into the soil and formed part of medieval cropping cycles.

The oil can be used for cooking, industry or fuel, and was even the main power for some lighthouses in the nineteenth century.

8 JUNE | DOG ROSE

'I know a bank where the wild thyme blows, where oxlips and the nodding violet grows, quite over-canopied with luscious woodbine, with sweet musk-roses and with eglantine.' (From *A Midsummer Night's Dream*, William Shakespeare, 1596.)

The wild rose. The plant of a thousand verses. Pain and pleasure intertwined. The dog rose and its close cousins, briar and eglantine, provide a perfume to induce any passing Titania to sleep.

Dog roses crop up in nearly every hedgerow, sometimes scrambling through the shrubs, or spilling out across a field. They have fierce thorns and large, five-petalled flowers, which vary from pink to white, but all have rich butter-yellow centres.

They are the plant of troubadours – a silver dog rose was the second prize for the French medieval 'Floral Games' which celebrated poetry. They are anything but humble. Contemplate one and smell its scent: a domesticated rose is not a patch on one of these.

9 JUNE | BANDED DEMOISELLE

If you have a slow-flowing river or pond nearby then you may well receive a visit from this stunning damselfly.

They flit a bit like a butterfly, but with delicate lace wings crossed with a deep black band, so that they almost flash in the sunlight. The long, thin body shimmers metallic blue in the male and emerald green in the female.

Damselflies differ from dragonflies in that they fold their wings along their back when they land rather than holding them stiff and straight.

They will be hunting for a pond to lay eggs because, just like a dragonfly, they spend most of their lives as water dwellers – two years underwater for a few weeks of freedom in the air.

10 JUNE | MARMALADE HOVERFLY

If Paddington Bear was an entomologist … this would definitely be his favourite insect.

It's worth getting to know this one simply because of its name. It looks like a miniature wasp and you will find it hovering above flowers on any sunny day. Like many hoverflies, it has a beautiful patterned body: sharp, rigidly symmetrical bands of black and yellow.

It's not an accident that it looks like a wasp. Mimicking something that stings and tastes horrible is a great evolutionary survival tactic.

Hoverflies are common and don't sting. In fact, they are really useful. They are the gardener's friend – their larvae eat aphids and keep them in check. They are also one of our great pollinators and love hunting for nectar on small-flowered plants like marjoram.

Once you have noticed Paddington's favourite you will start to see some others – there are 250 different hoverflies to get to know if you are keen.

11 JUNE | COMMON SPOTTED ORCHID

Health warning: this next item could afflict you with orchid fever.

In the early nineteenth century the discovery of exotic orchids led to a dangerous, and sometimes life-threatening, frenzy of collecting and trading in orchids, known as Orchidelirium.

But orchids are not just something for rainforests. You will almost certainly have one growing near you. The common spotted orchid is the one to look for, I think. It has sword-like leaves (a bit like a bluebell) covered with black spots and a spike of pink-purple flowers clustered around the stem. Each flower has the characteristic almost humanoid orchid shape.

Orchid hunting has a well-earned reputation for danger: orchid hunters have been captured by guerrillas, eaten by tigers, or simply never found again. Near where I live the principal hazard is that orchids seem to like growing on verges and the entrances to roundabouts – which is not quite in the same league, I feel.

12 JUNE | HOGWEED FLOWER

By mid-June, the cow parsley in the verges gives way to another 'umbelliferous' plant. *Umbelliferous* – a plant with flowers like a sunshade – now there is a word to conjure with.

Hogweed is taller and stouter than cow parsley. It has larger leaves and a much sturdier stem. Insects absolutely adore the flowers. Bees park up on a hogweed flower and spend an age gorging on one sip of nectar after another. You may find one populated by mating soldier beetles, as if on a big round bed.

It is regarded as a weed of hay meadows, but I think that is unfair; it adorns a June roadside very well. Occasionally you will find a stem where the flower has been bitten clean off – roe deer like hogweed too.

13 JUNE | GREEN WOODPECKER

Now is a great time to see a yaffle. Green woodpeckers live up to their name and are far from shy. In this season they are out and about on any short turf-hunting for food and teaching their youngsters how to behave.

Unlike their black-and-white cousins, green woodpeckers spend a great deal of time on the ground. They have an incredibly long tongue, which they use to hoover up ants, their major source of food.

You might hear one before you see it: they have a laughing call that is easy to learn, and a distinctive, looping flight that reveals a yellow flash.

14 JUNE | HERB BENNET

You will note that in general I have avoided Latin names, but this one deserves a mention: *Geum urbanum* – it's a town plant.

Herb bennet looks a bit like a buttercup, with loose-petalled yellow flowers which don't wholly cover the green-fringed calyx beneath. It's another of those plants that forms seeds with a Velcro-like hook to be spread by animals or woolly socks.

Gardeners may well think of it as a weed, but our forebears regarded it as a blessed herb, and the common name probably comes from a corruption of its old name *Herba benedicta*, St Benedict's herb.

It has clove-scented roots that were once worn as amulets to provide protection from evil. It was believed that a man wearing such an amulet was immune to the poison of beasts.

15 JUNE | BIRD'S-FOOT TREFOIL

We always called this plant 'granny's toenails' because of the shape of the half a dozen seeds that it bears. It's in the pea family, hence the tiny pea-like pods.

Bird's-foot trefoil is a wonder plant for insects. Dozens of different pollinators flock to the small yellow flowers as soon as they open. Some have a reddish tinge, which gives rise to one of its other common names, 'eggs and bacon'.

It is a plant of meadows and downland, and it crops up in lawns as well. There are all sorts of trefoils, vetches and vetchlings in the same family (clover is a relative too), but this is the plant to learn first.

Many butterflies love the plant, but it is most closely associated with the common blue, which lays its eggs mainly on bird's-foot trefoil. Few things are more pleasing than a blue-winged butterfly on a yellow ground.

16 JUNE | MEADOW BROWN

This is one of the most common butterflies of all, cropping up just about anywhere with long grass, and usually resting with its wings tightly closed. In the right place, you may see hundreds of them – a knee-high cloud of butterflies.

It's easy to overlook them, but they are far from mundane. They have an orange flash and large eyespot near the fringe of each upper wing, sometimes with smaller spots beneath.

The eyespot is another example of a genetic adaptation to trick predators: the flash of an eyespot may serve to scare a predator away. An eyespot on the edge of a wing distracts an attacker; a butterfly can survive a peck on the wing much better than a peck to the body.

17 JUNE | CUCKOO SPIT

June is marked by cuckoo spit on the stems of grasses. This has nothing to do with cuckoos, although the name may come from the fact that it appears around the same time. Instead it is produced by a tiny, plant-feeding insect called the froghopper or spittlebug, which has developed an ingenious strategy of wrapping itself in 'bubble wrap' while feeding on the juices in a plant stem.

In mainland Europe froghoppers are responsible for the spread of a bacterium called *Xylella fastidiosa* that has devastated olive groves in southern Italy. So far froghoppers in the UK are free of the disease, but if you do see cuckoo spit, make a note, and this could help track the disease should it strike.

Froghoppers also have a superpower – according to Professor Malcolm Burrows, head of zoology at Cambridge University, they are the jumping champions of the natural world, with the ability to exert a force of more than 400 times their bodyweight to launch themselves into the air.

18 JUNE | RINGLET

You will probably have passed it by, but do stop and notice a peaceful little ringlet butterfly.

They look pale brown and nondescript in flight, but when they settle you will see that the undersides of their wings are sleek, beautiful and adorned with half a dozen white-rimmed black eyes.

Ringlets are butterflies of long grass and you have a good chance of seeing them wherever you can find some: twitching around between tussocks, dropping eggs between the grasses as they go.

19 JUNE | MEADOW CRANESBILL

This is the bright blue flower that can be seen alongside roads in summer. It likes a chalky soil, and if you are in the right part of the country then whole verges are adorned with it.

It's a geranium with five petals, a cousin of herb robert as well as numerous garden plants. It has pale, pencilled lines on its petals and a dozen or so dark stamens at the centre of its flower.

For me this is the plant of summer homecoming, welcoming you as soon as you hit the back roads.

20 JUNE | WILD STRAWBERRY

Eating a wild strawberry from a stony bank is one of the joys of summer. About now you might begin to notice the white flowers and spreading runners of the host plants.

They crop up in thin-soiled places, quarries, old railway lines and chalky banks. If you have ever visited a farm to pick your own strawberries then you will recognise them – the leaves and fruit are miniaturised versions of the commercial variety, with three-lobed leaves and tiny, seed-clad fruit.

William Morris produced a beautiful print inspired by the 'strawberry thief' – a song thrush eating a strawberry – so if you do want to come and eat one in June, be aware that you may have some competition.

21 JUNE | SUMMER SOLSTICE

My solstice is marked by the sunset point on a distant blue hill.

For the whole of the first half of the year, I rush out to look at every decent sunset and mark the sun on the horizon as it marches northwards from its westerly midpoint in March. This evening marks the end of the advance. Thereafter the sunset tracks back to the west and south until the year turns again in December.

Watching nature reveals how much the movement of the sun matters to the wildlife around us. Trees have different lichens on the sunny side of their trunks to those on the shaded side. Anthills have a warm side and a cold side, with vegetation to match. Hollows that hold frost are different to slopes that catch the sun.

This is the idea of aspect – the angle of a slope and the direction in which it faces makes a huge difference to the things that will live and grow there.

Little wonder then that the solstice mattered so much to our forebears that they wanted to measure the year with marker stones and monuments.

22 JUNE | DUSK

If you can live through a winter in the high latitudes then the reward is the never-ending summer evening. Not only is it a magical experience, it is also the source of some of our most beautiful words: twilight, dimpsy, evengloam.

Midsummer is the time to sit outside as late as you can – with blankets or coats on if necessary – simply to watch the light change and settle. In Shetland this time of year is the 'simmer dim', and it doesn't get dark at all. I once spent a whole night on a Fair Isle clifftop, singing tunes and learning to look at things, staring due north as the sun set to the far north-west, tiptoed beneath the horizon shining upwards on to the clouds and then rose again to the north-east.

As a child I felt that time stretched out at this time of year, with street cricket matches extending into the near-darkness. Normal rules don't apply: succumb to a small dose of midsummer madness.

23 JUNE | PIPISTRELLE BAT

Just after sunset is when to look out for bats.

Stand still, let your eyes adjust and look up.

They fly too fast to follow, whistling past your head and into the shadows, but a glimpse is all you need – everyone knows the distinctive shape of a bat's wings.

Bats are harmless; a tiny flying mouse that hoovers up insects at night. They fly and hunt in a remarkable way. If you listen to them with a bat detector you will hear short squeaks of sonar that enables them to fly at high speed without hitting anything.

How do I know it's a pipistrelle bat? I don't, but they are much the commonest, and I am happy just to know it is a bat. They all squeak different tunes, so one day I may point a bat detector at it and find out. For now I am just happy to marvel.

24 JUNE | MEADOWSWEET

'No one left and no one came,
On the bare platform. What I saw
Was Adlestrop – only the name

And willows, willow-herb, and grass,
And meadowsweet, and haycocks dry'

(From 'Adlestrop', Edward Thomas, 1914.)

Meadowsweet: the defining plant of the elegy about late June, when everything seems to pause for breath and lie still. The poem was written by Edward Thomas from a memory about this day – 24 June 1914 – and has all the more power because of what followed later that year.

Meadowsweet is a ditch plant, about the same size as cow parsley, mentioned above, with a froth of creamy white flowers. It does have a sweet smell, with a hint of almond I think, and historically was used to flavour mead.

It still grows by the station at Adlestrop, where the land lies wet even on a June day and the trains have long since ceased to stop.

25 JUNE

YELLOW UNDERWING MOTH

Sometimes nature will come to you. If you leave your windows open with your lights on, then moths will probably follow. You will be able to find them sleepy in the morning, like teenagers after a party. I like the yellow underwing moth – something common enough to turn up in just about any house at this time of year – the name is all the description required.

Moths are probably wise to come inside at night, as the aforementioned bat is very fond of them. Some moths can hear the sonar of an approaching bat and go into elaborate flight manoeuvres. If you are feeling mean then you may be able to startle your sleepy moth into life by shaking your keys at it, which can cause a similar effect.

26 JUNE | SELFHEAL

Time for a picnic – lying on a freshly cut lawn is one of the joys of summer. You may start to notice things you hadn't seen before: a surprising number of botanical discoveries have been made when plant hunters have stopped for lunch.

Lawns contain a set of plants that can tolerate regular browsing or cutting in just the same way that plants on the tideline have adapted to cope with regular doses of salt water. As long as you don't fertilise or interfere with a lawn, over time the process of mowing creates a distinctive 'vegetation community'.

Selfheal is one of those plants that loves a lawn as long as it isn't cut too often. It has low-growing purple flowers that look almost like a miniature orchid and, as the name suggests, was once, and for some cultures still is, an important ingredient in herbal medicine.

27 JUNE | COMMON CATSEAR

There are lots of things that cunningly impersonate dandelions, and you may notice one of these in your nearest patch of lawn.

It is perfectly fine to call all yellow flowers like this 'dandelions'. They comprise a very large family of plants, and even experts sometimes struggle to tell a hawksbeard from a hawkweed or a hawkbit.

At this point you might discover whether you are a 'lumper' or a 'splitter', according to Darwin's description of nature observers. Lumpers like big groups of similar things and think there are only 800 types of hawkweed; splitters, on the other hand, emphasise differences, and think there are easily 10,000 different species and subspecies.

Whichever category you are in, I think it is worth learning to distinguish a dandelion from a catsear. Catsear flowers look like someone has taken a dandelion and snipped the edges straight with scissors and then added a couple of notches for luck.

On close inspection (do pick one) catsear doesn't have a hollow stem, nor does it stain your fingers with bitter juice. They have hairy leaves not smooth; the stem is wiry not hollow. They form tiny little clocks with their seeds rather than picturesque dandelion clocks.

28 JUNE | CATERPILLAR ON A NETTLE LEAF

This is why you left those nettles growing! If you hunt around the tops of tall nettles, you might find a cluster of tiny caterpillars.

They may be 'woolly bears' – the larvae of the beautiful garden tiger moth – or perhaps the equally exotic peacock butterfly.

Small tortoiseshell butterflies are fussier, preferring young nettles, so if you want those then a spring nettle chop to induce new growth can be helpful.

You may even be helping to create the next generation of commas, a butterfly that lights up an August evening. Whatever caterpillar it is, you can help them by leaving the nettles a while longer.

29 JUNE | GRASSES

Go back to your childhood, squeeze a broad blade of grass between your thumbs to make a grass trumpet … and blow. Failing that, hunt around the pavements for some barley arrows to pick and throw like darts.

Grasses are everywhere in June but I suspect that most of us barely reflect on how much we depend on them. Many of our staple foods – wheat, barley, oats and rye – are types of grass, and yet we often don't give their parent plants much attention.

You needn't to be able to identify all the different grasses to be curious about them, although there are few enough common ones that you can begin to get to know them. They have the unusual property of growing from their tip, so if you cut the grass it simply grows back again.

If you let grass grow long then not only will it flower, but it will also provide a tiny 'forested' landscape within which a multitude of insects, voles and mice can live. So, if you have a big enough area of rough grass then you will attract kestrels, bats and maybe even barn owls. If you mow or plough every inch then you won't. That is why field edges and margins matter.

30 JUNE | GRASS NAMES

Brown bent · common bent · bristle bent · creeping bent · marsh foxtail · meadow foxtail · marram · sweet vernal-grass · false oat-grass · meadow oat-grass · downy oat-grass · tor-grass · quaking grass · upright brome · crested dog's-tail · cock's-foot · tufted hair-grass · wavy hair-grass · smooth finger-grass · sea couch · common couch · tall fescue · sheep's fescue · red fescue · viviparous fescue · Yorkshire-fog · creeping soft-grass · crested hair-grass · perennial rye-grass · purple moor-grass · common reed · annual meadow-grass · smooth meadow-grass · sand cat's-tail · common saltmarsh-grass

JULY

Colour hints of seedhead-brown and pale straw-stem start to pervade the early summer palette of yellow and green.

Pavement cracks and walls fill with unruly pink herb robert and stout mallow. Fields tinge poppy red. Ants take flight. It is the season of picnics and festivals and summer meadows.

In a warm year, the air fills with dust and pollen. Rain brings sweet relief and summer scent.

Left: Ivy-leaved toadflax.

1 JULY | POPPY

The field margins are dressed with blood-red poppies as if to mark the anniversary of the Battle of the Somme.

There is a whole suite of plants that like disturbed ground and some, like poppies, are particularly associated with cultivation. Modern seed cleaning and sprays have made many of them rare, but you may still see red poppies scattered around fields at this time of the year.

In 1916, the ground in northern France was in the midst of a second summer of ground disturbance: the futile ploughing of soil and loss of human lives. This tragedy provided the perfect conditions for poppies and cornflowers.

We think of the First World War as something defined by grainy, black-and-white images and mud. Yet the visiting war artist William Orpen was staggered by an intense burst of colour, the like of which he had never seen:

'Never shall I forget my first sight of the Somme in summertime … no words could express the beauty of it … White daisies, red poppies and a blue flower, great masses of them stretched for miles and miles.' (*An Onlooker in France 1917–19*, 1921.)

2 JULY | LIME TREES BUZZING

Inside St James's Church, Piccadilly, in London there is a beautiful piece by the master sculptor Grinling Gibbons, which dresses the north wall of the spare white church and has been bathed in choral music for more than three centuries.

The sculpture is made of the best carving wood, the timber of the fine, pale lime tree. You will have seen a lime tree – they are the towering trees of parklands and avenues with big, heart-shaped leaves.

In July this statuesque tree, up to a height of 100ft (30m) or more, is draped in tiny, heavy-scented cream flowers, and it seems as if every bee and fly for a mile around has come for a meal.

Stand underneath a lime tree in July and you can bathe in a different kind of music – the whole tree is abuzz. Pause for a moment and soak up the music of the bees.

3 JULY | SWIFTS FLYING

The swifts have fledged and it is time for flying lessons. Ten or 20 birds are screaming around the same circuit in town like a group of teenage joyriders.

They knife through the evening air in a ragged gang, shouting to each other with high-pitched squeals as they take each tight bend. You can barely see their heads at all – at this speed swifts are four-fifths wing and one-fifth tail. They glide and dive with barely a flap and change direction with the faintest flick of a feather.

They tend to follow the same circuit over and over again as if the buildings really are some kind of street-racing circuit. If you can find the right pub garden you can enjoy the best nature experience of the summer, without even leaving your seat.

4 JULY | WALNUT TREE

If you can find a walnut tree then it should not be too late to pick a few green walnuts to make that most unusual of pickles. I am a bit lukewarm about it, but my father is a fan so best to prepare a jar for Christmas.

Walnut trees have smooth, grey bark and great big leaves like a giant ash. In spring the flowers drop from the trees like an infestation of huge green caterpillars.

Here walnuts are ornamental trees, sometimes planted in parks or gardens. In France, you may find tall walnut orchards, producing fruit and walnut oil. I can only imagine standing in the native walnut forests of Kyrgyzstan in central Asia beneath a whole host of these beautiful trees.

5 JULY | MEADOW

A traditional meadow in July is a wondrous sight. Once, meadows were 'shut up' after the end of March to allow the grass to grow, and the animals were allowed to return after the hay cut in late July or August. The result is a flower-rich hay meadow – one of the great natural wonders.

Across most of the country meadow grass is now mostly cut in May to be pressed into silage for animal feed. This is good economics, but bad news for birds that nest on the ground, and for the flowers that set seed in June.

If you can find an uncut hay meadow in July then you can bask in an Impressionist blaze of summer colour, while watching insects go about their business.

Happily some farmers are rediscovering the benefits of a flower-rich meadow and are grazing animals in little 'mobs' while letting the flowers set seed elsewhere. It turns out that a rich diversity of food types is much better for animal health as well as for wildlife.

6 JULY | COMMON BLUE

Most butterflies and moths have the most wonderful, evocative names: comma, lappet, rustic, merveille du jour. By contrast, whoever was responsible for naming the common blue started, and immediately won, a competition for the most underwhelming lepidopteran moniker.

There is no excuse for this, as the common blue is anything but underwhelming: it is as bright and exotic as any rainforest insect.

It has perfect Mediterranean-blue wings, with a tiny white margin. The backs of the wings are dotted with white and black spots with an orange fringe. Even the female butterfly, which is brown, shimmers blue in flight.

If you see a blue butterfly in summer, then it is most likely a common blue. The other blues are much scarcer and more local. Adonis, chalkhill and silver-studded blues were also clearly named by someone else …

7 JULY | ROSEBAY WILLOWHERB

Railway lines can be surprisingly colourful places and some plants specialise in colonising them. Buddleia – a magnet for butterflies – is one. Rosebay willowherb is another, with its tall spikes of purple flowers that put down roots in any patch of stony waste ground.

During the Second World War it was called bombweed, as it rapidly turned bomb sites into floral displays and became a symbol of resilience.

Rosebay willowherb is another adopted plant. In North America it is called fireweed as it springs up soon after a forest fire. For Native Americans it once had numerous practical uses, from food and medicine to cord-making.

Here, it competes with railside graffiti for attention as the brightest thing on display: bombproof, bright and cheerful.

8 JULY | SUMMER RAIN

After a spell of hot weather, the cool drenching provided by a sharp summer storm seems to fill the air with a sweet scent.

Yet, this is not just our romantic imaginations at play. The smell of clean air and wet earth yields a very distinctive aroma, which goes by the name of 'petrichor'.

A storm stills the summer dust and washes the air clean of pollen. The atmosphere seems immediately cleaner and sharper. But, there is something else happening as well: rain stimulates bacteria in the soil to produce a molecule called geosmin, which we humans are really good at detecting.

The splash of a raindrop releases this into the atmosphere. There really is a smell of summer rain.

9 JULY | IVY-LEAVED TOADFLAX

My grandmother used to grow snapdragon plants in her front garden. She would pick them to place on our fingers so that we could 'talk dragon' to each other. For that reason our little wall snapdragon, properly named the ivy-leaved toadflax, always makes me smile.

It grows in walls and seems to need only the tiniest crack to make a home. It has little cymbal-shaped leaves and smart purple and yellow flowers.

It's a true rock plant, thought to have been introduced to the UK from Italy as early as the mid-seventeenth century, and it arrived just in time to take advantage of a craze for walled gardens. Since then it has escaped and you will doubtless find it on a wall near you.

10 JULY | WORMWOOD

'Mealy' is the word most frequently used to describe this large, greyish silver plant that appears on road verges with its heads of rounded white seeds.

It is known as wormwood, a name to inspire fear and wild imaginings.

You may think that a name like this may be somewhat melodramatic for a scruffy grey plant that grows by the roadside. Think again: you can make a substance called wormwood oil from this plant and this is a core ingredient of emerald-green absinthe, the drink of choice for the wild imaginings of Hemingway and Picasso.

11 JULY | GORSE SEED

In January, the occasional gorse flower is the brightest thing around on a grey day. By late July most of the gorse bushes are once again decked with only a few flowers; most of the bush is strewn with pea-pod gorse seeds.

The seeds crack sharply in the heat of the sun, for gorse is a lover of heat. If you burn a bush to get rid of it, it will resurrect phoenix-like as soon as you turn your back. Gorse likes nothing better than to grow in the ashes of burnt gorse.

By the coast, gorse bushes are often the tallest things on a cliff-top, often topped by a songbird – a linnet, yellowhammer or perhaps even a stonechat – just letting you know that you are on their turf.

12 JULY | HAWTHORN SHIELD BUG

Brush through a hedgerow this month and you may emerge carrying a shield bug. This one is a hawthorn shield bug – neat and green.

These are little sap-sucking insects about half an inch (1cm) long and are shaped (needless to say) just like a knight's shield. They can fly if they open their wings, but most of the time they walk around on six stout little legs. They also go by the name of stink bugs as, if disturbed, they leave a foul, sticky trail.

There are 200 different types of shield bug. Hawthorn bugs vary from green to bronze, but the others come in a range of colours.

13 JULY | REED-BED

'Since I was cut from the reed-bed, I have made this crying sound.' ('The Reed Flute's Song', Rumi, *c.* thirteenth century.)

It is not just Rumi, the Persian poet and mystic, who gave reed-beds a primal association. When Prometheus stole fire from the gods, he spirited it homeward inside the stem of a reed. The Mesopotamian reed-beds inspired the idea of the Garden of Eden; Abraham was born among the reeds.

Get close to a reed-bed and it is easy to see why they are associated with stories. They seem to talk constantly. Susurration – the sound of reeds – is more of a whisper than a cry. In summer it is accompanied by the electric chatter of reed warblers and the yelp of a water rail.

In the UK, when conditions are right, the common reed creates huge banks of pale vertical stems, head high or more. Imagine what a place this is for wildlife: lots of water and places to hide, with nice boggy ground to impede any predators.

So, get back to your roots. It may require a special trip, but a visit to a reed-bed in summer is restorative.

14 JULY | MALLOW

Mallow is a purple flower that is reminiscent of a geranium. It is another summer plant of field edges and waste ground. It has stout stems and cheese-button seeds which, I recall, make great ammunition in an alleyway plant-throwing battle. Our most common variety grows very quickly into a bushy shrub that can be as tall as a child.

Mallow is mentioned in the Old Testament Book of Job as a poor foodstuff: the leaves, stems, fruits, and seeds of the mallow are all edible. The round seeds look like little loaves of bread and the name of the plant in Arabic is 'khubez', derived from the word 'khubz', which means bread.

During the siege of Jerusalem in 1948, one species of mallow played an important role. Mallow soup, rich in iron, was one of the dishes cooked by the Jewish people in order to survive.

15 JULY | ST SWITHUN'S DAY

St Swithun's day does indeed feel like a make-or-break point in the British summer.

Swithun himself was a popular Anglo-Saxon bishop, but it is not terribly clear why he qualified for sainthood – to me his sole miracle of repairing a basket of broken eggs doesn't quite make the grade.

He is better known for his love of the open air, and the fable runs that if the weather is set fair on 15 July then it will hold for the remainder of the summer, whereas if the day is wet then August will also be a washout.

There is perhaps a grain of truth here – late summer weather sometimes becomes stuck in a pattern around this time.

16 JULY | HUMMINGBIRD HAWK MOTH

Now, these creatures are not common, so they really have no place in this book.

Yet they are such an exotic visitor – one of the fastest insects around and they really look like nothing else – so let's make an exception. They are also visiting the UK more and more as our summers have become warmer.

There are lots of hawk moths but this one behaves like a hummingbird: hovering stock-still in front of a flower with its long, camouflaged body tilted sharply downwards. By completely separate evolutionary processes the moth and the hummingbird have devised the same strategy for feeding from flowers while in flight.

Hummingbird hawk moths visit us from southern Europe and deserve a special mention as an omen of good luck. While the D-Day ships were sailing south in June 1944, they encountered a swarm of these unmistakable insects heading in the opposite direction.

17 JULY | WILD CARROT

This is an altogether more upmarket version of cow parsley. It is an inhabitant of dry road verges, cliffs and banks. It is also distantly related to our domestic carrot.

It has stiff, grey-green stems, and beneath the flowers there is a beautiful curl of leaflets that set off the flat cream flower heads.

Wild carrot looks fabulous next to a boulder on a cliff-top, with gorse flowers and blue sea behind. Yet it also adds immense grace to a roundabout or road junction.

18 JULY | BUFF-TAILED BUMBLE BEE

I am not very good at sitting still, but a sunny afternoon is the time to spend a few minutes watching the bumble bees. They are lovely, gentle, busy little insects: constantly feeding on nectar, using a long tongue to extract it from their flower of choice.

Bumble bees do not look like a creature designed for flying, and a full stomach will only give them about 40 minutes of flying time. The buzz comes from incredibly fast-moving wings, flapping at 200 beats per second. They very rarely sting.

This buff-tailed bumble bee has very handsome yellow-and-black stripes with a pale tail. I can also get close enough to see bright yellow 'baskets' of pollen attached to each hind leg.

Within a couple of weeks the annual cycle of the bumble bee colony will have finished for another year and there will be fewer bees around.

So, just like W. B. Yeats in his poem 'The Lake Isle of Innisfree' (1888), I am going to spend a few minutes 'alone in the bee-loud glade' storing up a memory of a perfect summer day to last me all through the winter.

19 JULY | COMMON SHREW

There is a dead shrew on the path. It is dark grey and soft with a pointed nose. Something has caught it and learned that they are not very nice to eat at all. There are nearly as many shrews as there are people in the UK (40 million, according to the Mammal Society), yet you don't see them very often.

Life is fast for a shrew; their hearts can beat up to 20 times a second. The smallest shrews have a faster heart rate than any other mammal on Earth. They have incredibly sensitive whiskers and the ability to stun their prey with tiny, venomous fangs (don't worry, they are harmless to us).

If you are lucky enough to see a live one you will note that they are all of a twitch, full of busy, jerky movements. So would you be if you had to eat your bodyweight in food each day in order to survive.

20 JULY | PARACHUTING SPIDERS

While travelling across the south Atlantic on HMS *Beagle* in 1832, Charles Darwin noticed that the ship was covered in tiny webs full of spiders. 'I caught some of the Aeronaut spiders which must have come at least 60 miles,' he wrote in his diary.

July is the time to notice our native spiders using exactly the same tactics, creating a 'parachute' made of tiny silk threads, which can carry them hundreds or even thousands of miles to find new sources of food and new mates.

It has now been discovered that spiders are not just using wind to get airborne, but they also have the ability to detect and use electric fields, which can allow them to fly even on a still day.

21 JULY | PAINTED LADY

Late in July, the buddleia bush is decked with the arrival of our visiting desert butterfly – the painted lady. They look as if they would be more at home on the scrubby Saharan desert fringe of Morocco, with vivid orange wings topped with a pattern of black and white.

A wave of painted ladies emerges from this part of Africa in the spring. Following the breeze and navigating by the sun, one generation after another travels north, laying their eggs on thistles. These then hatch, pupate and emerge to continue the journey of their parents.

By late July the first of these reach our shores, and every ten years or so there is a population explosion where clouds of these desert butterflies come to join the peacocks and red admirals on any nectar source that they can find.

It has now been discovered that some of these butterflies will make the arduous journey back south in October, and that others cross the Sahara twice on a 7,500 mile (12,000km) journey – the longest migratory flight of any butterfly.

22 JULY | BLACK KNAPWEED

These are wonderful purple plants, a mainstay of July meadows, sometimes called hardheads because of the sheathed and armoured base to their flowers.

Their Latin name, *Centaurea*, is for Chiron the centaur from the Greek myths, who made a herbal poultice with knapweed to cure a wound caused by an arrow. I think that was quite an achievement with those hooves.

The flowers used to be eaten in salads (although they must have been a bit tough) and to make potions, but I suggest you leave them as food for the insects.

The various species of knapweed are loved by butterflies and hoverflies, and they flower for much of the summer. The flowers are also popular with one of our lovely summer moths: the red and black six-spot burnet, which can often be seen lazily sucking nectar from the flower heads.

23 JULY | SMALL TORTOISESHELL

If the sun is out then we should be counting butterflies. Some of our early butterflies will have already come and gone, but by this time the big butterflies of summer are out in force.

Small tortoiseshells are fabulous summer butterflies. They have orange wings with an electric-blue fringe. The upper wings are adorned with a black-and-cream check which adds to the exotic effect.

Painted ladies reared on desert thistles are all very well, but I think that you will have to agree that they are not as glamorous as our homegrown, nettle-loving small tortoiseshell.

24 JULY | SCABIOUS

This is the sky-blue flower of late summer. It has a broad, flat flower head made up of many little flowers each sitting atop a rough, hairy single stem.

In the UK in late July scabious flowers seem to be visited by a strangely implausible insect with antennae three times as long as their bodies.

The name scabious makes these flowers sound unappealing and it probably derives from the roughness of the stem. However, they are anything but unappealing, and every insect in the neighbourhood will agree. They also used to be prescribed as a treatment for skin ailments – although one suspects this was not hugely effective.

25 JULY | WILD PANSY

You may think of a pansy as a plant for blowsy, old-fashioned borders, but there is a wild version too, the heartsease, which once grew so widely that it is said one could walk across a whole tract of Shropshire treading on one plant after another.

The wild pansy is tiny, as delicate as a violet, and if you look closely you may find it growing on the edge of a sandy field with its purple and yellow petals.

The name is derived from the French 'pensée' – the thinker's plant – but it is romantic thoughts that are said to spring to mind. In *A Midsummer Night's Dream* it was the juice of this flower that caused Titania to fall instantly in love.

Maybe I should pick one …

26 JULY | FIELD BINDWEED

Bindweed is a really hard plant to love if you are a gardener. It is a vigorous climbing vine that winds stems corkscrew-like around any plant that it touches. It climbs, it forms mats underneath stones, it has brittle roots that regrow from the smallest fragment. It is a weed par excellence.

Our field bindweed is in the morning glory family (Convolvulaceae) and if you can bear to let it flower you will see

why – it has huge, white-and-pink, cup-like flowers to complement its triangular green leaves.

Bindweed definitely has a fairy-tale appearance. It can take over a whole area and conjures up visions of the giant beanstalk as it grows. Fittingly, the flowers received a mention by the Brothers Grimm who called it 'Our Lady's Little Glass' – a flower used by the Virgin Mary for a drink of wine after helping a passing wagoner.

27 JULY | EMPEROR DRAGONFLY

Dip your toes in a pond in summer. In July, particularly after a dry spell, water is a magnet for wildlife.

While you sit by the pond, you may be visited by a giant dragonfly: the emperor dragonfly is a huge insect in apple-green with a blue-striped tail and stiff gossamer wings, and it restlessly scouts around any patch of water at this time of the year.

Dragonflies march to a different drum. They have compound eyes with thousands of lenses that can see incredibly quickly – they have a reaction time of 30 milliseconds – meaning the dragonfly will have reacted and acted

before we even notice that there was something to react to in the first place!

They move in a quick-quick-slow manner – darting and then hovering as they hunt for mosquitoes and flies to eat.

While they are giants of the modern world, these creatures are tiny compared to their ancestors from 250 million years ago: a dragonfly fossil from the coal measures of Derbyshire is more than 1½ft (0.5m) across.

28 JULY | FLYING ANT

Not many insects get a mention on the weather forecast. Yet, during the summer of 2019, huge clouds of flying ants were shown moving eastwards on the interactive weather map. There were so many ants in the air that the radar was mistaking them for raindrops.

At this time of year, colonies of our common black ant are on the move. They produce huge numbers of large-winged virgin queens and smaller-winged males. This is the mating season and the flight is a mechanism to ensure not only that colonies can establish elsewhere, but also reduce the chance of inbreeding.

When the conditions are right, on just a few days each year, there is an explosion of flying ants from beneath paving slabs and cracks in the concrete, off to found a new citadel beneath the soil.

29 JULY | VIOLET GROUND BEETLE

Learn to love a ground beetle. My favourite is the big violet ground beetle that marches rapidly over the soil in flower beds and verges.

Ground beetles (and their cousins the rove beetles) are a good thing. We are lucky enough to have over a thousand varieties. They signal that the bottom end of the food chain is in good order, and they also keep the pests in check. You can encourage them by leaving leaf litter in borders and providing little wood piles for them to hide in (and by avoiding accidentally poisoning them with slug pellets, of course).

Violet ground beetles have a metallic purple sheen to their wing cases and would fit nicely on a 50p piece. They are avid eaters of slugs and worms, but completely harmless to humans.

30 JULY | ST JOHN'S WORT

St John's Day has long since passed, but beside the stone walls in the village of Kelmscott in Oxfordshire grow some yellow flowers that, for me, are one of the signs of late summer.

St John's wort is a flower that always seems to face the sun. It has five yellow petals and stamens like the sun's rays. It has all sorts of uses, but at Kelmscott it was one of the plants used as a natural dye.

We can imagine that William Morris, the father of the Arts and Crafts movement, may have collected St John's wort here. He hated chemical dyes and I like the idea of him trying to produce his own, dyeing his arms up to the elbows in the process.

31 JULY | TEASEL FLOWER

Teasels are in flower in July. Purple flowers spiral upwards and downwards in two bands around the stretched globe-shaped spiked flower-heads.

Their spiky stems are clasped by long, prickly leaves that trap rainwater and unsuspecting insects, just like a carnivorous plant. Indeed, some research suggests that a good store of drowned insects does indeed help teasels to thrive.

Teasels are the flowers once used for teasing apart strands of wool and for combing the nap of fabrics. In the early textile industry, clusters of flower heads would be fixed to frames for this purpose.

I can't see them without thinking of the goldfinch – the teasel finch that loves them, which will doubtless be back here in autumn to eat the seeds.

AUGUST

August: golden and hazy-remembered season of harvested fields and visits to the seaside.

The birds have disappeared for a summer rest, so throw open the high windows and treasure the sleepy morning moths as you cajole them outside.

Invite someone to help find a rockpool. Throw pebbles together into the water. Find somewhere dark enough to lie outside and watch for a meteor.

Sit for a moment in the park. Summer is running down and there is no time to lose.

Left: Rock pool with anemones and starfish.

1 AUGUST | LAMMAS/LUGHNASA

Rather than 12 months of the year, many of our oldest cultures split the year into eight parts. There are the four big markers of the turning of the year: the two equinoxes of equal length day and night, plus the two extremes of light and dark. Spaced roughly in between these were the 'quarter days'. The beginning of August is lammas, or for the Irish, 'lughnasa'.

Lammas is corn-cutting time: another reason for a ritual, a feast and a dance. It was traditional to cut a blessed loaf into four quarters and place each of them in the corners of the barn before bringing in the crops.

If you watch nature then it seems to make much more sense to mark time by the movement of the sun in this way than it does to split it into arbitrary, 30-day moon cycles. The Romans have a lot to answer for.

2 AUGUST | WILD OATS

'The first sheaves of oats on the hillside shone yellow in this morning's sun, and the stubble crinkled underfoot on the way up to the oak wood, where the late shoots covered with young light green leaves made every branch appear from the distance as though it were tipped with gold.' (*The Guardian Country Diary*, 2 August 1919.)

Early August seems unchanging and still. In summer the tall stems of wild oats tower delicately over fields of crops. The flowers – for that is what they are – are dozens of drooping, pointed pairs of grassy seeds held together in a neat V-shape.

Oats were once one of our most important crops, but they are now grown less for food than they were. Nonetheless the wild oats linger on, disrupting the neatness of the wheat crops and filling any roadsides and field corners.

Not everything is sere brown. The oak trees throw out 'lammas growth' at this time of year. This is a second flush of new, bright green leaves, which stand out against the dark green lobed leaves below them.

3 AUGUST | HONEYSUCKLE

Honeysuckle scent creates a hypnotic air on a summer's evening. It's not for our benefit, it is there to attract helpful pollinating moths, but it is one of the sweetest smells of late summer.

Honeysuckle is the woodbine plant. It twines, always clockwise, around shrubs and trees sometimes so strongly that it twists the stem to which it is attached into a spiral shape.

It has long, cream-and-pink clusters of tubular flowers – the longest-tongued moths will have the best chance. Later these flowers turn to bright red berries that feed the birds in autumn.

4 AUGUST | FEATHER

Among the bracken on the floor of the wood is a long, narrow black feather with white spots along the side.

It's the feather of a great spotted woodpecker, something to take home as a memory of the walk.

At this time of year, it feels as if the birds have suddenly disappeared. After a frenzied spell of dawn singing and then some busy feeding of their young, our feathered friends are less apparent.

Part of the reason is connected to the feather on the floor: this is the peak time for birds to freshen up their feathers for the winter ahead. It is the summer moult.

Feather by feather, over the space of six weeks or so, many birds replace all of their feathers, ready for the winter ahead.

This takes a lot of energy, so August is a good time – the weather is warm, food is abundant and there are many bushy places to hide while you are having a 'bad feather day'.

Come September, the birds will all be out and about again. Meanwhile, I am off for another walk, hunting for the most special of all summer finds: a bright blue jay feather.

5 AUGUST | GRASSHOPPER

Listen to the sounds of crickets and grasshoppers. Even better, try to catch one gently in your hands for a close look – that will keep you occupied for a while as it is not easy.

Sixty-five million years ago, when a huge asteroid-induced extinction event killed 95 per cent of living things on Earth, these were one of the creatures that survived.

Look closely at these little locusts and it is easy to believe that they are ancient creatures.

They make a noise using a process called stridulation – rubbing a rough leg across their wings. It is the soundtrack of summer.

6 AUGUST | CRACK WILLOW

Crack willow trees line riverbanks and damp hedgerows. They have dark green, spearhead leaves with a silver-grey underside.

The tradition in many places is to 'pollard' them – chop all the branches off a little above head height to create a stump which throws out huge volumes of weavable willow stems.

They grow ridiculously fast on damp ground, and if left to grow tall they crack and split, as if living up to their name. New trees will grow from stems thrust straight into the mud, and in places you may see a whole hedge of willow where fenceposts have taken root.

The crack is also the sound of a summer cricket bat – hybrid willows are still grown especially for that purpose.

7 AUGUST | ROCK POOL

One of the things that you lose as an adult is the ability to easily imagine yourself shrinking and expanding like Alice after accepting the invitation, 'Drink me'.

Rock pooling is the way back in – after a few minutes you can lose yourself in a miniature landscape of cliffs, fjords, bays and shorelines.

This apparent similarity between large and small is common by the sea – the ripples in the sand look eerily similar to the ripples in the fair-weather clouds. This is not a flight of fancy – it is the underlying logic of the universe.

Unfolding symmetry – where similarities appear at different scales – is a product of the mathematics of fractal geometry. It is why the soapy whirlpool down the plughole looks curiously similar to a hurricane.

So, gaze into the looking glass of the rock pool awhile. It is deeper than you think.

8 AUGUST | SEA ANEMONE

In the rock pool you will see sea anemones – they will probably be tightly closed beadlet anemones, which look like someone has glued a jelly sweet to the rocks.

They are not stuck down, though: they can move, and if you hunt around you will find one that is open, with tentacles on display, stinging anything that passes to make a meal. It's clearly a good strategy because an anemone can live for as long as a human.

Other creatures make their home among the anemone tentacles as if hiding in the mouth of a lion. My favourite anemone – the snakelocks anemone, which is common on westerly shores – looks a bit like a shaggy lion's mane.

9 AUGUST | COMMON TERN

Among the gulls you may see something much more stately. The tern is the swallow of the sea: a grey-white, knife-winged bird with long tail streamers.

I prefer the Shetland name for them, 'tirrick', as it captures their sound as well as their shape. If you watch for a while you may see them fold their wings and dive headlong into the sea in search of sand eels.

They can be seen on a lake inland, but they really look at home skitting above white-topped waves. These are true ocean travellers, spending the summer in the UK, but travelling nearly pole to pole to spend our winters cruising the rich waters of the Southern Ocean.

10 AUGUST | STRANDLINE

The strandline is the ever-moving space where land ends and the sea begins. In this country we have some of the biggest tides in the world, and so the strandline moves further than in most other places. As the moon waxes and wanes, the tides grow stronger and weaker and the high-tide mark marches up and down the beach on a fortnightly cycle.

Just above the strandline you will find a few plants that can survive the occasional winter storm: sea kale, scurvy grass and oyster plant. The strandline itself is too variable for anything to take root, but it is alive with sandhoppers, springtails and the indomitable woodlouse.

This is a special place for things that like change and are happy to dust themselves down and start again twice a day. It can be messy, it's the place for flotsam and jetsam – things lost and things discarded – but it is full of life as well. In among the inevitable plastic I like to look for mermaid's purses, the egg capsules of sharks and rays, and also goose barnacles on old pieces of driftwood. One day I hope to find a whale bone, or a sea bean dropped from a tree in the West Indies.

11 AUGUST | SHELLS

Shell collecting is a gentle summer pastime. Sandier beaches will provide cockles, sometimes in perfect matching pairs, and perhaps razor clams. Rockier shores provide the purple haze of a million mussel shells, or the multiple colours of snail-like periwinkles.

In the seventeenth and eighteenth centuries the wealthiest in society would show off their money and appetite for learning by creating a 'cabinet of curiosities'. These might be filled with the exotic and unusual, or with an array of beautiful things.

As displays of wealth go, this is rather a charming choice – and many of the cabinets that survive feature shells as part of their collections, often from faraway lands.

I find that a shell beach has a similar effect to gazing into a cabinet: a mesmerising array of shapes and textures that make you want to pick things up and feel them.

12 AUGUST | KELP

In front of me on the shore is a giant seaweed trunk with long, air-filled fronds, still attached by a 'holdfast' containing bits of the rock on which it was once fixed.

Holdfast is one of the most fantastic nature words. The holdfast at the kelp's base forms a network of nooks and crannies, providing a home for hundreds of individual animals. Worms and crustaceans burrow into the gaps, anemones and sea squirts cling to its surface, and small fish use it for shelter. Larger fish, like lumpsuckers, often lay their eggs among the holdfasts.

Our seas are special places for kelp forests – on the Western Isles we have rocky shores where the kelp can grow to as much as 100ft (30m) in length. Forest is the right word for these; they sway in the waves rather than the breeze, create spaces for life in both the canopy of kelp fronds and the shaded sea floor. They hold huge amounts of carbon and are a nursery and hunting ground for fish and seals.

13 AUGUST | PERSEIDS METEOR SHOWER

If you are lucky enough to be able to find a dark sky then tonight is the night to wrap up, sit back and search the skies for shooting stars.

There is something miraculous about the fact that, each year, as regular as clockwork, our planet sails through a cloud of debris from a dead comet. For a couple of nights in August, if the skies are dark and clear, we are visited by a meteor (a shooting star) every minute.

The Perseids emanate from the constellation of Perseus, but you don't need to be a star sign expert to seek them out. Just find a seat that lets you lie back to avoid a stiff neck and look upwards in a northerly direction.

Sixty miles (almost 100km) overhead, pieces of space dust are burning up as they plunge into our atmosphere. Some are faint and you may only catch sight of them from the corner of your eye, but if you wait and watch you may just see a larger chunk burning up in a slow arc as it crosses the sky.

14 AUGUST | MOON JELLYFISH

Walk along the shore and the chances are that you will find a flying saucer – a jellyfish. You may find lots: a whole 'smack' of them.

Jellyfish have a whole host of reasons to go on a visit to see the Wizard of Oz. They have no bones, brain, or heart – yet they are one of the most successful creatures in the oceans.

The creature in front of you is most likely to be a moon jellyfish, with four circles arranged cross-like across its centre. This variety doesn't sting people but it is a very effective predator of plankton.

They may look like flying saucers and be named after the moon but, jest not, jellyfish are one of the creatures that have travelled into space. American scientists sent this very species of jellyfish on a space shuttle trip to study how zero gravity affects their ability to tell up from down. Needless to say, they came back with serious vertigo.

15 AUGUST | MARRAM GRASS

The surface of the sand is hot, but as soon as my bare feet sink into it, there is cold sand beneath. I remember crossing sand dunes as a child, running all the way there hunting for a glimpse of sea. I remember the return journeys too, endless trudges as if lost in the Sahara with no water.

The scratch of the grass sparks a memory too: this is marram grass, the wondrous sand dune plant.

It is named *Ammophila* – 'the friend of the sand' – and it has long underground roots that bind the sand together. On a dune their leaves dominate the scene with a straw-green fringe.

Marram grass is successful because of an adaptation of the leaves that allows it to survive on very little water – just like a desert plant. The leaves are waxy and curl inwards and the stomata, the openings present on all leaves, are deeply hidden to minimise water loss. It was so useful to coastal communities for thatching, fuel and fodder that the Scottish parliament had to limit harvesting in the late seventeenth century for fear that the dunes would blow away.

16 AUGUST | DUNE

Marram grass and dunes work together because the grass doesn't entirely stop the sand from moving – and dunes need to move to stay alive.

On a windy day, you can see sand grains whipping across the surface of the dunes, forming a heap around any tiny obstacle. Each one is a miniature dune – they form, grow, move with the wind and then in turn are blown away.

Moving landscapes like this have their own distinctive communities of plants and animals, which shun anything so dull as a static home. There is a special type of *Euphorbia* – the sand spurge – that thrives here. You might see a skittering lizard diving into the marram. And at dusk the yellow, sagging flowers of evening primrose cast a scent across the sand.

17 AUGUST | SHORE CRAB

Take a sideways look at the world and take someone crabbing. It's a great way to get to know our clever little shoreline friends.

Shore crabs are the most common crabs that you will catch. They are armoured and fierce like a Greek warrior, but once you get to know them you will find that they are not as vicious as they first appear. They may give you a sharp nip with their powerful front claws, but don't take it personally.

All crabs have ten legs, two of which are large front claws for catching their prey. They also have a hard shell, which they have to shed as they grow out of it through a process called moulting.

All good crabbing sessions end with a crab race down the shore, a sideways sprint back to the safety of the water (with maybe a detour under a stone or two).

18 AUGUST | STARFISH

You may find a live starfish in a rock pool, or a dead one washed up on the beach.

They are extraordinary creatures, with seawater instead of blood, and the ability to regenerate their own arms if they happen to lose one.

Our common starfish usually has five arms, each with an 'eye' at either end that allows them to navigate their way across the rocks and move towards a source of food.

Starfish have a tough outer skin that makes them less attractive to predators, and the absence of a brain (just like a jellyfish) doesn't seem to get in the way of being successful.

19 AUGUST | PEBBLE

Pebble-hunting is addictive. When I was a child, we used to visit my grandmother near the steep flint beaches of east Kent. The daily ritual was a walk along the shore, hopping over the barnacle-clad groynes, hurling pebbles into the surf which collected them and swept them back up the shore with a roaring crash.

Each time, my grandmother would give me the task of finding a pebble with a hole all the way through it to bring home for her. Weaknesses in the flint mean that occasionally you find a pebble formed like this, sometimes with a tiny stone pushed into the gap.

Pebbles are the halfway point in the aeons-long journey of stone from tall cliff to tiny-grained flat sand. Further along the coast on Dungeness the sea has mapped a part of this process, by rigorously sorting pebbles from fist-sized boulders at one end to fine shingle at the other.

I never thought anything more about my little task until many years later, clearing out the house after my grandmother died, we found a jar containing all the pebbles that I had collected as a child.

20 AUGUST | SUNFLOWER

Above Rhossili Bay on the Gower peninsula in Wales, sunflowers light up an ancient field system. Like many things in nature, sunflowers look as amazing up close as they do massed across a late summer field. The flower heads are made up of perfect, intersecting spirals that will later become a beautiful seedhead.

What connects a sunflower, a pine cone with an ammonite's shell and a dragonfly's wing (and the proportions of the Acropolis, for that matter)?

The answer is the mathematics of nature.

Each seed in a sunflower head is rotated at the same angle (137.5 degrees) from its neighbour. As each new seed is formed, this angle is repeated, creating a tightly packed spiral pattern.

The maths is simple, all based on a series of numbers noticed by Italian mathematician Fibonacci in the early thirteenth century: the next number in the sequence is the sum of the previous two: 1, 1, 2, 3, 5, 8, 13, 21, 34 and so on. From this sequence arises the angle that forms an ammonite's shell and the 'golden ratio' that makes the Acropolis the model for buildings to this day.

Discuss: does knowing this make a sunflower more beautiful or a dragonfly more remarkable? Take it or leave it.

21 AUGUST | SLOW WORM

Lay a piece of tin – corrugated iron is good – in a spot that catches the morning sun and you may discover that you share your home with a slow worm. Failing that, you may find one if you turn the compost heap.

They shimmer in the light as a greyish silver, or soft coppery pink, and they have bright black, blinking eyes.

They are lizards, not worms, and they are not really that slow. They are small, powerful little creatures that do a sterling job hoovering up slugs in the garden.

22 AUGUST | LARGE WHITE

There are several largely white butterflies, but the large white is definitely the most common.

If you grow vegetables you will know the caterpillars of this butterfly, as they turn up on any cabbage plant in August as a cluster of black, white and yellow.

Large whites have black-tipped upper wings and are rather handsome, despite the fact that everyone dismisses them as 'cabbage whites'. The other two common white butterflies are smaller, but quite similar in appearance: the green-veined white – lover of garlic mustard – is probably prettiest, with bright green undersides to its wings.

23 AUGUST | OAK SPANGLE GALL

Try hunting for spangles. I don't mean the tongue-mangling sweets from the 1970s. Oak spangles are caused by the larvae of a tiny little gall wasp. You will be unlikely to see the wasp, but you may see the galls that their eggs create on the underside of oak leaves.

Some look like little doughnuts and others more like silk buttons, depending on the species of wasp.

Oak spangles always remind me of how much is going on in nature that I can't see or don't understand. That's how it works – for every new thing you learn, you discover ten things you didn't know that you didn't know.

24 AUGUST | HEATHER

'The chimneys of the old mines pointed starkly; early moths blurred the heather-bells.'

(Virginia Woolf, *Jacob's Room*, 1922)

The whole hillside above seems to have turned purple overnight. At the end of August heather flowers dress the high hills in a purple cloak.

A heather bell is the flower of late summer uplands and lowland heaths. It's a plant of good luck, and – as someone married to a Heather – it has always been lucky for me.

This is a plant of poor, soggy, acidic soils. From Woolf's far-west tin-mine country to the East Anglian Brecks and from Hardy's Egdon Heath to the Scottish mountains beloved of Burns, this early autumn flower is one of the sights of the season. Turn off the path, feel the heather on your ankles and keep your eyes out for a white heather sprig – the luckiest heather flower of all.

25 AUGUST | BUDDLEIA

This is the queen of butterfly plants. In August these tall bushes are draped with long, conical purple flowers that are a magnet for butterflies.

It is a native of central China that has become as commonplace as a takeaway restaurant, especially along railway lines and on wasteland.

At this time of year buddleia becomes a playground for our big three common butterflies, peacock, red admiral and small tortoiseshell – sometimes joined by rarities and visitors such as fritillaries or comma.

There is nothing better than approaching a buddleia and seeing a flight of butterflies spin off in a loose circle before settling gently, higher up the bush.

26 AUGUST | PARKLAND

'Humans are a woodland edge species', or so a friend once observed. Whatever the truth of this, we certainly seem happy with our backs to a tree looking across a plain – as if surveying the savannah for threats or prey.

Perhaps that is why we love parkland. A true park is an artificial creation made by enclosing deer – a practice that has been happening since at least medieval times. The resulting landscape of big, spreading trees and close-cut turf was copied in a more formal way by the eighteenth-century landscape designers and later by those designing city parks.

Parklands are special not just for their large old trees, but for all the fungi, insects and creatures that are associated with them. Above all, though, they are places that people love: a home for our species.

27 AUGUST | JAY

While wandering across a summer parkland, you may come across a tiny oak sapling far from the nearest tree. This is most likely the work of another of the oak trees' partners in crime – the pink-feathered jay.

Jays are little crows and they share the singing ability of their cousins – i.e. very little. As you start to listen to bird songs you may notice the clattering call of a jay in woods or parks, where it likes to hang out.

The Latin name for this bird, *Garrulus glandarius*, translates as 'noisy acorn eater' and that is a great summary. The noisiness is only matched by a voracious appetite for acorns. From round about now, a jay goes into a frenzy of acorn-gathering and so this is a good time to see them.

It is thought that a jay can hide up to 5,000 acorns in a season, transporting them in their gullet to be buried and eaten later. They are good at finding them again, even in snow, but the oak tree only needs them to forget a few …

28 AUGUST | SILVERWEED

I am trying to make a habit of walking barefoot more in summer. It's good for your body and it educates your feet.

Some plants are better to walk on than others, but the leaves of silverweed are best of all, and this time of year they seem to take over the grass. They are small, creeping buttercups, with silver, almost fern-like leaves that form a soft, flat pad.

The roots are edible too, and in the Scottish Isles the plant is known as 'an seachdamh aran' – one of the seven breads of the Gael – once a core part of the local diet before potatoes became common in the mid-eighteenth century.

These plants, along with strawberries, belong to the *Potentilla* family – the 'little powerful ones' – and they seem to be easily strong enough to put up with a trampling. It is said that Roman soldiers picked silverweed leaves to use as padding in their sandals.

29 AUGUST | BRACKEN

We have a family story that one of our ancestors was an immigrant French glassmaker. I don't know the truth of it, but it is called to mind every time I see a sea of bracken.

Remember how to identify bracken – this is the fern that has branches. But what does it have to do with glass?

With enough heat, you can make glass from the simple ingredients of ashes and sand. Some of the glass from the early Middle Ages is called fern glass – 'verre de fougère' – because the ashes of bracken plants were used in its manufacture. A bit of bracken ash in the mix produced a finer-quality glass.

You need to cut a lot of bracken to make a small amount of ash, so this is not something to do unless you can make something special, but the bracken-clad landscapes of Cannock Chase in Staffordshire and the Weald of south-east England had all three ingredients for the early glass industry: wood for heat, plenty of bracken and as much sand as you need.

Bracken is beautiful as well as useful, particularly the young leaves, which open with characteristic fern fiddleheads.

30 AUGUST | PINEAPPLE WEED

At the gate that enters the field, I can suddenly smell pineapples.

This is pineapple weed: an introduced plant that has successfully made its home here. Not only does it look like a tiny pineapple, but when crushed the flowers also smell of the fruit.

In late summer it fills gateways, roadsides and field edges, especially where the soils are light and sandy. Here it may be accompanied by another type of daisy – the scentless mayweed – and the other weeds of cultivation: groundsel, shepherd's-needle, chicory and poppy.

31 AUGUST | SEA AREAS

After a few days by the seaside, I will have to survive on memories for the winter ahead. I shall rely on the poetry of the shipping forecast. Each word conjures up a different image filled with colour and sound.

Dogger A flat, grey North Sea with a whole civilisation beneath.
Wight Chalk-tooth cliffs rising from a blue-gum sea.
Lundy Seabirds wheeling in Atlantic swells.
Fair Isle Friends, walls, the tang of sheep on a salt breeze.

Here is my recitation for winter:

Viking · North Utsire · South Utsire · Forties · Cromarty · Forth · Tyne · Dogger · Fisher · German Bight · Humber · Thames · Dover · Wight · Portland · Plymouth · Biscay · Trafalgar · FitzRoy · Sole · Lundy · Fastnet · Irish Sea · Shannon · Rockall · Malin · Hebrides · Bailey · Fair Isle · Faroes · South-east Iceland

SEPTEMBER

Dew-clad, web-strewn, fruitful September.

The seas are at their warmest from the summer heat. Rivers steam mist in the cool mornings. Cobwebs cloak the lawns. Wasps decide to become annoying.

The equinox, the day of equal light and dark, marks harvest time. The hedges and fruit trees are heavy with fruit and still full of leaf, and it's the season to gather crops and cook for friends.

Left: Blackberries.

1 SEPTEMBER | BLACKBERRY

Taste a blackberry. Even better, forage a few and make a crumble.

You might need to taste fruit from a few different bramble plants as some are definitely sweeter than others. The bramble is another of those plants that has hundreds of variants, so a bit of experimentation is required until you find one that suits your palate.

The red fruit are unripe, so you need to be selective, and there is only a moment or two when a blackberry is perfect before it begins to sag.

Children love picking blackberries – it must be the combination of risky thorns and sweet fruit. Many birds and animals love them too, so you have competition from blackbirds and foxes.

At this time of year there is enough for all, free food from those forgotten places where brambles thrive. So get blackberrying and invite some friends round for tea.

2 SEPTEMBER | WOODY NIGHTSHADE

If you are inclined to worry then learning about wildflowers is not necessarily helpful for your nerves. All around us there is an array of poisonous plants, many of them very common.

However, as a child it was this particular plant that we chose to frighten ourselves with: it was what we called deadly nightshade.

In fact we were referring to the plant called woody nightshade and it is not as poisonous as its rarer, deadly cousin. It has five purple, curved-back flower petals around a central yellow spike and it scrambles through hedges and beside ditches.

After the flowers come rugby ball-shaped berries: first green, then yellow, through orange and finally turning red. The plant also goes by the name of bittersweet, which it is said describes the taste of the poisonous berries. I certainly wouldn't try it.

3 SEPTEMBER

BANDED SNAIL

In among the long grass you may find the shells of our stripy snail – they go by a variety of names, but banded snail will do for now.

It so happened that Darwin chose to travel to the Galapagos Islands to look at the impact of natural selection on the bills of finches. But he could have stayed here and looked at snails instead.

The colour and number of stripes of banded snails is determined by genetics. The same species of snail can vary from yellow to rose-coloured and brown. Equally, some snails can have up to five stripes and some have none at all.

What determines which type of banded snail occurs local to you? The forces of natural selection here involve temperature control and camouflage from our snail-smashing friend, the song thrush.

Dark is good camouflage in some places, but in hot weather it is a disadvantage as the shell heats up uncomfortably. Stripes are good camouflage in pale, dry, grassy late summer, but can be conspicuous early in the season.

Where I live, yellow with lots of stripes seems to be the dominant uniform of choice. It blends well with the long, pale grasses.

4 SEPTEMBER |

ELDERBERRY

The lemon-scented elderflowers of June have given way to wine-dark elderberries that stain the ground beneath.

The shrub itself looks really scruffy by this time. The branches tend to bow as they grow and the elder responds by throwing out straight, vertical shoots, which makes it look like it needs a good haircut.

Elder has an enduring reputation as a magical tree. The leaves of the tree were once hung in doorways to ward off evil spirits and the berries have long been associated with healing.

It turns out that the berries do contain all sorts of things that help fight colds and viruses, but you will need to cook them first. Elderberries do make a nice country wine too.

5 SEPTEMBER | WASPS

The wasps are being really bothersome.

For most of the summer, these worker wasps have been fully occupied feeding the larvae in their papery nest. Now their work is done they are like teenagers with nothing to do – accidentally annoying. They are on a sugar frenzy, off to find any sweet thing they can to replace the larval milk that they have got used to drinking.

They are less likely to bother you if you sit still. So, take a breath, summon your inner calm and try to remember what wasps are good for.

It was this kind of Zen-like pondering that led to the discovery of paper. Around the first century BC, a Chinese monk noticed how a wasp made the finest paper nest from peeling off and mashing up fine layers of wood. If you have ever found an old wasps' nest you will see exactly the source of his inspiration.

Wasps are great pollinators too and play a huge role in maintaining the balance of nature in your garden, eating huge numbers of spring and summer insects.

So they are irritating, useful and beautiful – but you are allowed to put a glass over them until you have finished your picnic.

6 SEPTEMBER | RAGWORT

'Ragwort thou humble flower with tattered leaves. I love to see thee come and litter gold …' ('The Ragwort', John Clare, 1832.)

The ragwort is still in flower in September, bringing light to verges and wasteland with late summer colour.

Ragwort has developed a bad name and I think is in need of some rehabilitation. Our common ragwort is a native plant and it is beautiful.

It has a reputation as being poisonous, but it is by no measure the most poisonous plant around – quite a few of the plants in this book would kill you if you ate a few leaves or berries, but you would need a truckload of ragwort.

In any case, grazing animals don't tend to eat it as it tastes horrible, but it is a problem if found in hay, and for that reason horse owners are rightly wary.

The residents of the Isle of Man have a different perspective. For them it is the 'cushag' – the flower of the island.

7 SEPTEMBER | DEW

Even if awoken from a very long sleep, one would only need to step outside on a dewy, apple-strewn lawn in the morning to know that it is September. Early in the morning the mists of September mark out every hollow in the ground and transform the landscape.

This is the dew-clad month. The sun starts to lose its heat and a clear night chills rapidly. Once a surface cools sufficiently (to the dew point – which varies with the weather), any water vapour in the air will condense to form droplets known as dew.

In the Namib desert, dew is the only water around and a specially adapted type of beetle survives solely on the moisture that condenses on the surface of their body. Here they would drown in September, especially after a still clear night, under which dew forms best.

This truly is the 'season of mists and mellow fruitfulness' ('To Autumn', John Keats, 1819). No phrase captures a month better.

8 SEPTEMBER | SPIDER SEASON

'Each bird and stone, each roof and well, feels the gold foot of autumn pass; each spider binds with glittering snare, the splintered bones of grass.' ('Field of Autumn', Laurie Lee, 1947.)

The dew on the grass and the low sun reveals that everything suddenly seems to be covered in spiders' webs.

This time of year is 'spider season' and, whether you like spiders or not, please spare a minute to notice the intricacy and beauty of a dew-beaded web.

Each species of spider spins a different type of web to catch insects for food. The spider's silk is one of the most remarkable substances known: incredibly light, but much stronger than a steel thread of the same diameter.

It's also peak time for spiders coming into your house, and it will usually be a male spider as they are off on the hunt for a female. According to recent research the most common time to see a spider is during the evening at around 7.35pm – but that may reflect more on our habits than theirs.

9 SEPTEMBER | RED ADMIRAL

Red admiral butterflies are out and about.

The Greeks thought that the butterfly represented the soul and Psyche, the goddess of the soul, is often depicted with butterfly wings. That is certainly how a red admiral in autumn makes me feel.

This butterfly sports the colours of fire: velvet-black wings and a splash of crimson and white. It's another of our summer visitors. Some red admirals may appear in spring, having spent a winter in hibernation, but most of them flow in from southern Europe and even North Africa as the summer progresses.

By September we have a second wave of butterflies that have hatched out and fed on our nettle leaves, and they keep the company of wasps in feeding on fallen fruit.

10 SEPTEMBER | BADGER PATH

You will be very lucky to see a badger. They are nocturnal and extremely shy. Despite the fact that there is a large population in the UK, it is still unusual to see one, except perhaps jogging surprisingly quickly in front of your car along a country lane.

The paths to a badger sett, on the other hand, are easy to find once you know what you are looking for. Badgers are creatures of habit and tend to follow the same routes each day. The area near a sett, where up to 20 of these black-and-white creatures may live, is criss-crossed with a path network. On wet ground you may see a claw print as they have climbed a hill. Or you may find a cluster of hairs caught where they have squeezed under a fence or through a thorn bush.

All roads lead to the sett, with has many different holes making up past and present entrances, and a 'latrine' connected by a tunnel further away. Leave the sett be – they are asleep!

11 SEPTEMBER | FAIRY RING

Look across a patch of closely mown grass and you are likely to see signs of fairy rings: 'the green sour ringlets whereof the ewe not bites'. (*The Tempest*, Act V, Scene I, William Shakespeare, c.1610.)

Pause a moment before stepping inside the circle: legend has it that you may be forced to dance indefinitely by the witches or fairies that created this magical ring.

It's easy to see why these have magical associations. They look as though they have been drawn out by someone: a circle of dead grass surrounded by a circle where the grass grows strongly.

In September, the source of the mystery is revealed when a fairy ring of mushrooms often appears. It is a fungus of course. Each year the ring grows and expands and some of the largest are centuries old and can grow hundreds of feet across.

12 SEPTEMBER | DAMSON

Damson jam, what could be more quintessentially English than that? Quite a lot of things, it would seem, as the damson is another gift from invaders who made their home on these islands.

Near me, deep in the woods, are the remains of a small Roman villa. If you gently scuff up the first autumn leaves you will find a mosaic floor. Damson stones are one of the things that have been found in places like this. If you always thought that these little plums were English then can I offer the chance of a Damascene conversion? Our humble damson is actually the 'damascene plum' – a fruit most likely brought here from Syria by the Romans.

Early in September, a damson orchard is heavy with purple fruit. You may also find damsons in the hedgerow, as there are other hybrids of plum and sloe that also go by the name of damsons or bullaces.

13 SEPTEMBER | COMMA

These are the butterflies of a warm September evening. They are widespread but you never seem to see more than one or two at a time. They are yet another of our nettle-loving butterflies.

They are also masters of disguise, with beautiful, ragged-edged wings with a white comma marking on the back. At rest the butterflies look just like a dead autumn leaf, and they also have a chrysalis that looks just like a bird dropping.

In flight, in the late afternoon sun, they make rapid figures of eight, catching the light with wings of orange-and-black chequers.

14 SEPTEMBER

GREY SQUIRREL

I know that I shouldn't, but I can't help but love grey squirrels. Our native red squirrels are, of course, the good guys in this scenario, but in my neck of the woods I have to make do with greys. It is impossible not to be charmed by them.

This time of year is mainly occupied by manic food-storing activity – a quick shimmy up the walnut tree to collect a winter meal and then a race across the garden to find a place to bury it.

They are pretty fat at this time of year – and the irony is that this may turn out to be a source of competitive disadvantage. In some parts of the country the pine marten is starting to return and it turns out that it can coexist alongside red squirrels, who are light enough simply to wander to the end of the branch when it appears. The same is not true for the chunkier greys, who are too heavy to sit on a thin branch and instead have to make themselves scarce, leaving a helpful niche for the reds. So it may be that the return of a vanished predator is one of the keys to the renaissance of the red squirrel.

15 SEPTEMBER | HAZELNUT

The hazel trees are refusing to acknowledge that autumn is around the corner. The fresh, felt-covered branches are throwing out more huge leaves of pale green to add to several feet of summer growth.

There are a few whole hazelnuts on the floor among the many cracked open by squirrels. These are also known as cob nuts, with pale, plump, unhardened shells poking out from the fringy blanket of a green coat.

Hazel trees can be cut to the stump again and again. They simply throw out more and more straight shoots, which can be used to weave fences around borders or left to grow thick into a Druid-style walking stick.

They are my favourite of all trees, useful, indomitable and wise.

16 SEPTEMBER | GATEKEEPER

This is the first butterfly that I can remember learning about, during a long, hot summer when I was seven years old. One of them used to lurk in a cluster of brambles in the alleyway by the back gate and I was delighted to hear that it was so appropriately named.

If you watch butterflies, then it is a general rule that if you don't know what it is then it is usually a meadow brown. Gatekeepers can easily be confused for their commonplace cousins, but they are smaller and much more handsome. They have a small eyespot and orange wings with a broad brown border.

I later learned that gates are not an essential part of their habitat requirements, but they do love an autumnal bramble patch.

17 SEPTEMBER | SYCAMORE SEED

'Under the coole shade of a Siccamore
I thought to close mine eyes some halfe an houre,'
(*Love's Labour's Lost*, Act V, Scene II, William Shakespeare, 1598.)

Sycamores are hard done by. If you have an opinion about them then I suggest that it is time to revise it. You will know a sycamore. They have leaves just like the Canadian maple, which by this time of year are often spotted black with the tar spot fungus.

In September, you can clearly see part of the reason for the sycamore's success – they have a secret seed dispersal weapon. The seeds, called samara, come in pairs and are fused together into a boomerang shape. When released by a breeze they spin outwards, spiralling away from their parents.

They may or may not be a native tree (this is the subject of some debate), but like a lot of opportunist plants, they are the subject of vehement attempts to remove them. This is a shame as they support huge volumes of insects through their nectar-rich flowers and in the crevices of their scaly bark. I prefer the name Celtic maple – it sounds rather grander and honours their ability to thrive in the wilder corners of these windswept isles. Spend a minute trying to catch a descending seed as they helicopter towards you – I bet you can't catch one.

18 SEPTEMBER | FIELD MAPLE

Once you have got to know a sycamore seed, then you may also notice a slightly different seed that has the same tactic.

The field maple is the native cousin of the sycamore and it also produces pairs of helicopter seeds. In the case of the field maple, the seeds are set in a line opposite one another, rather than at an angle.

Field maple is a bit of a forgotten tree. You most often see it cut harshly like a shrub in a hedgerow, although it can form a handsome tree given enough space.

It also has five-pointed maple leaves like a sycamore, but the lobes of the leaves are much more indented. In autumn these can turn vibrant orange and red.

19 SEPTEMBER | FIRST STORM

The Met Office has recently adopted the charming habit of naming our big winter storms. Any time from now, we are likely to be visited by a swirling mass of cloud with a name beginning with 'A'.

Autumn tilts the Northern Hemisphere away from the sun, making the nights longer and the North Pole cool faster. This also brings the jet stream – the high-altitude currents of air that drive our weather and our storms – squarely over our heads.

Autumn storms have a noticeable pattern. First the skies are covered with a flat, high, grey cloud, then the wind picks up and turns south followed by heavy rain. The back edge of a storm is often marked by a sharp edge of cloud, a cold front, by which time the wind has turned to a cool north-westerly.

The first autumn storm blasts tranquil summer into a mess of fallen fruit and leaves, although in September most leaves are still green enough to hang on and shake themselves dry for another day.

20 SEPTEMBER | ROSEHIP

My neighbour, who lived in the house next door for 70 years, once told me about being given days off school to go and gather rosehips for the war effort. Not only did she get a day off, but she got a sixpence as well.

Rosehips are the red-orange fruit of the dog rose. They are rich in vitamin C and were used to make rosehip syrup at a time when we needed all of the gifts from the hedgerow that we could get.

We used to use them for less savoury purposes. The white pith from a rosehip is 'itching powder' and was one of the weapons of childhood, along with a barley dart and a pea shooter made from an elder twig.

21 SEPTEMBER | FLY AGARIC

This is the red-and-white toadstool of fairy tales. They are quite common, but they look as if they belong to hallucinations.

Lots of toadstools (or mushrooms – there is no difference) are not poisonous, but this one definitely is. There are at least a couple of thousand fungi species in this country, so if you want to start learning them, this is a good place to start.

Tales that this mushroom was taken to drive the Viking berserkers to a hallucinogenic frenzy turn out to be questionable, but the fly agaric is definitely something that inspires dreams – whether it is Beatrix Potter placing toads on toadstools, or Lewis Carroll imagining them as a seat for a pipe-smoking caterpillar.

22 SEPTEMBER | RIVERS

Who owns the river? We know that land can be owned, but can you really own a river? We all depend on them for drinking water. Surely they are something that we should hold in common for the benefit of all?

They are the arteries of the land and in many cultures rivers are sacred for that reason. They are beautiful as well as useful.

My memory of a river is hunting for sticklebacks and bullheads behind what seemed like an enormous waterfall, but can't have been more than a knee-high break in the stream. Later on we would swim in the Upper Thames beneath the weir, occasionally interrupted by the electric-blue flash of a kingfisher.

Whoever it is that owns the river, they tell a story about the way that we look after the land, and in my imagined future they all run clean and gravelled, fish-filled and with mayflies dancing.

23 SEPTEMBER | AUTUMN EQUINOX

Today is another turning point of the year. Just as at the vernal equinox in March, the days and nights are equal length. Tomorrow is the start of the long nights of winter.

Equinox, Michaelmas and harvest are all different ways of marking this balance point of the year. This is a time for settling your debts and counting your blessings. I don't like the arrival of the darkness, and part of the reason for writing this book is to cope with the descent into winter from this point.

I find that making a plan at equinox time is a good start. The period to the shortest day now breaks into two neat, six-week parts.

From now until Hallowe'en we have the richness of autumn with its colour, fruits and fungi, and the new arrivals of winter – the geese, swans and fieldfares. From Hallowe'en until Christmas there are just a few weeks of cold austerity to fill with the appreciation of stems, bark and frost as well as fire and parties. And then on 21 December, the year turns and every day brings growth and light. This makes things so much easier!

24 SEPTEMBER | SWALLOWS ON A WIRE

At this time of year the swallows line up on the telephone wires as if forming an orderly queue for the long trip back towards the south.

It is feeding time; flights of swallows skim low over any water they can find, or skirt hedges hunting for insects. The swallows need all the food that they can get before an epic migration.

Some will have already started the long journey back to Southern Africa to spend the winter, travelling 200 miles (320km) a day across France and over the Pyrenees before a hazardous trip across the Sahara.

My heart selfishly wants to urge them to wait another week or two, but my head says that they should set off now – while the weather is good and they are strong – to give them the best possible chance of being back here next year.

25 SEPTEMBER | WOOD MOUSE

There is a wood mouse about.

I know this because it has left little markers to stake out its territory, just like a cub scout making direction arrows with sticks. A twig has appeared where none was previously. That chewed hazelnut definitely wasn't there yesterday.

Wood mice are the only animal known to waymark their territory with objects in this way (apart from humans, of course).

This time of year is a good time to see them. They are busy gathering food to store up for winter. They hop rather than scurry, and they are prodigious munchers of hazelnuts. You can tell if a nut has been chewed by a wood mouse from the neatly shaped hole in the top of the shell, rather than the less subtle grey squirrel, which just cracks them straight in half.

26 SEPTEMBER | SPEAR THISTLE

Thistledown fills the air.

At this time of year you can see why thistles are so successful. They are another plant with seeds that fly on the breeze and prosper quickly on patches of disturbed ground.

Goldfinches peel off thistle heads as we approach. The odd late purple bloom still attracts insects and butterflies.

They may be the bane of farmers and gardeners, but I am on the side of Eeyore, famously a lover of thistles.

27 SEPTEMBER | MILLIPEDE

Turn over a log, or move a dustbin, and you may encounter a millipede curled up into a neat spiral beneath, perhaps accompanied by a woodlouse or two.

Millipedes are another of those creatures that turn the wheel of life. They are 'tidiers-up', consuming decaying vegetation to make leaf mould and soil.

What is the difference between a millipede and a centipede?

They don't have a thousand legs – somewhere between 40 and 400 is more usual – and they move their bodies in undulating waves as they walk in military step.

There are countless varieties and several different strategies for survival, each of which is reflected in the animal's shape. Some look like bulldozers and have short legs for pushing through leaf litter; others have pointed heads for tunnelling; and then there are the 'wedgers' with a flat head for opening up crevices.

28 SEPTEMBER | HARVEST FESTIVAL

Tucked snugly into the steep cliffs of North Cornwall sits a tiny driftwood cabin high above the Atlantic waves.

This is Hawker's Hut, built by the nineteenth-century parson Robert Hawker, as a place for a smoke, a moment of contemplation and a bit of writing.

Hawker was not just a poet. In 1843 he was responsible for the first modern harvest thanksgiving service when he invited his parishioners to a celebration in the church at Morwenstow. This was the reinvention of an ancient ritual: a time for giving thanks that the harvest had been brought in and the stores were full. For hundreds of years this has been the time to honour the last sheaf of corn from the year before and hope for a favourable year next year.

Today is harvest festival day – a day to be thankful for the food that we eat.

29 SEPTEMBER | ANGLE SHADES MOTH

Butterflies are scarce now, but there are lots of moths about.

This is an unmistakable and distinctive moth with pinkish-brown markings. It sits with folded wings which make it look just like withered autumn leaf.

The adults are attracted to light so I think that is why this one has appeared at the window. I have seen them out and about in the day as well, resting in the open on the fence opposite.

I know my butterflies, as there are only a few to learn, but every time I see a moth like this I think to myself, 'I must get to know my local moths'. That's a resolution for next year.

30 SEPTEMBER | MOTH NAMES

The names of moths give an insight into the minds of the eighteenth-century naturalists who gave most of them their names. We may no longer have footmen (apart from the Royal Family) or clad ourselves in ermine, but the names seem to capture not just the moth, but also the spirit of an age.

Here is a selection of my favourites:

Mother Shipton · pretty chalk carpet · old lady · yellow barred brindle · burnet companion · burnished brass · puss moth · figure of eighty · vapourer · silver Y · varied coronet · vine's rustic · white ermine · reddish light arches · pebble prominent · cream spot tiger · square spotted clay · pygmy footman · chimney sweeper · barred straw · the annulet · lunar underwing · nut-tree tussock · oak eggar · obscure wainscot · peach blossom

OCTOBER

'October 26, 1783. Wonderful and lovely to the imagination are the colours of our wood landscapes at this time of year.' (*The Natural History of Selborne*, Gilbert White).

October can be gentle and fine. A few days of still frost turn the leaves amber and deep red. On the high chalky ridges, beech woods take on an ethereal orange tone.

Overhead, the V-shaped lines of winter geese flying in remind us that further north the winter has arrived already. The last of the swallows head hurriedly southward, hunting for winter warmth.

Yet October can be wild too, settling into a pattern where storms trundle in from the west with barely a pause between, before the arrival of Hallowe'en – the start of the dark days.

Left: Shaggy inkcap mushrooms and bracken.

1 OCTOBER | GEESE

Geese! A long, ragged 'V' of birds writes their way south and westward across the grey page of sky. Some of these birds will have flown this way every October for 30 years, often with their lifelong partner. Mr and Mrs Goose are coming home for winter.

This is an ancient ritual. Autumn is about arrivals as well as departures, and these geese have come from Siberia, Greenland, Spitsbergen or the high Arctic tundra. They are escaping the frozen wastes to spend the winter on damp, lush, British grass.

They may be barnacle geese, whose autumn appearance was once so mysterious it was believed that they emerged from the folded, blue-grey goose barnacle that you sometimes find on long-lost pieces of driftwood. Or, they might be white-fronted geese, once common along parts of the Severn Vale.

It doesn't matter. Just call them geese. Save the identification for another day. Nothing lifts my spirits more as the days begin to shorten. Look up, welcome some old friends coming back in search of wet meadows and mild winters, honking hello as they fly past.

2 OCTOBER | SALT-MARSH

We are blessed with these amazing places around much of our coast and it is not only the geese that love the low, flat landscape of a salt-marsh.

Salt-marshes are the dank places of Dickens novels, 'dark, flat, wilderness … intersected with dykes and mounds and gates, with scattered cattle feeding on it'. (*Great Expectations*, Charles Dickens, 1861.)

They can look bleak, but spend any time near one and they will beguile you. They are neither land nor sea. They are a place of reflections and ever-changing light.

From above you can see the complex, brain-like pattern of channels that fill and drain twice a day, sheltering the coast from storms and providing a wonderful home for wading birds and geese.

If you are not already an addict then October is a great time to learn to love a salt-marsh.

3 OCTOBER | SWAN

There are other water birds flying south for the winter. You may see swans flying in as well.

If you do, then make sure that you stop and listen. They fly fast and straight, with necks held determinedly forward, and huge white wings that make a whooping sound with each flap.

Our mute swans, all protected by the Crown, spend the whole year with us. They have orange bills and don't tend to say very much. They adorn our rivers with graceful white necks and beautifully folded wings.

In autumn they are joined by two rarer, yellow-billed swans. It was the smaller of these, the Bewick's swan, that provided inspiration for the great conservationist Peter Scott who noticed that he could tell each individual visitor at Slimbridge from the unique patterns on their beaks.

Once you know, like Scott, that each swan is

part of a lifelong couple that come back here year after year from the Russian Arctic fringe, then you can't help but think about the world a little differently.

4 OCTOBER | NAVIGATION

How do these birds make their incredible journeys each year? For long-lived birds like geese and swans, there is the advantage that the youngsters can follow an experienced navigator.

But there is something else at play here. Some birds have a sixth sense, which gives them the ability to detect the Earth's magnetic field to help them navigate, and is thought to relate to a specific protein in their eye. This allows them to fly accurately along the same routes each year.

5 OCTOBER | GIANT PUFFBALL FUNGUS

The grassy common on the hill looks like someone has abandoned a whole load of white footballs in the night.

These are giant puffballs, another of our amazing fungi. It is tempting to give them a kick, but it is better to leave them for others to enjoy.

They feel leathery, just like an old football, and if you can find one that has split apart you will find a dense mass of mushroomy flesh.

Like most fungi, they reproduce by releasing microscopic spores into the air, and a puffball doesn't want to take any chances. The big puffball in front of me may contain a trillion spores.

6 OCTOBER | LADYBIRD

Apparently from nowhere, there are suddenly dozens of ladybirds huddled in the corner of the window frame. They are in defensive formation, like a phalanx of Roman soldiers armed with tightly packed shields.

It feels like the last dying day of summer and the ladybirds are in the air too. They are not really shaped like a creature that can fly, but they have more than a little poise when on the wing, unlike some of their other beetle relatives.

These are harlequin ladybirds and they come in many colours – black on red, red on black, yellow and cream – but they all share distinctive yellow-brown legs which are obvious in the low autumn sun through the window. They only arrived in Britain in 2004; they are native to the eastern part of Asia – Japan and Russia.

If you see a red one with seven spots then you are looking at something else. This is the original native seven-spot ladybird, wearing a red cloak like the Virgin Mary and with seven spots to mark her seven joys and seven sorrows.

Harlequin ladybirds are a source of sorrow to some – they eat other ladybirds – but today I take joy in their sheer abundance and array of colour.

7 OCTOBER | SLOE BERRY

The same place where you found blackthorn blossom in spring is now a very good place to look for sloes, the blackthorn fruit, as long as the birds haven't got there before you.

One of my favourite things is to pick a sloe berry and slowly rub the blue blush from the fruit with my finger to reveal the shiny purple beneath.

They taste like one of those tablets that you can't swallow, and when held in your mouth has a bitter flavour that robs you of saliva.

Yet, with a bit of work, you can extract the most delicious flavour from them. Now is a good time to make your sloe gin for Christmas, or sloe wine if you are so minded.

If you are organised you will be ready to offer up the perfect hedgerow Christmas present, sloe gin and elderflower tonic. Unbeatable.

8 OCTOBER | CRANEFLY

Everyone knows a daddy long-legs, the insect of early autumn, a great gangly thing with barely attached legs.

They end up inside our houses at this time of year, flying aimlessly across windows or getting stuck in spiders' webs.

They also go by the name of cranefly, and there are over 300 varieties in this country. At this time of year we see the common variety with a black-tipped tail, but earlier in the summer there are some more exciting ones around – including the tiger cranefly with brilliant yellow and black patterns.

9 OCTOBER | FIRST FROST

The first proper frost of autumn changes the scene. Some of the summer flowers that have been hanging on as the days shorten are suddenly reduced to withered husks.

Until now it has looked as if most of the leaves are still green, but overnight the frost seems to have changed that and I notice more yellows and browns among the canopy.

The average length of time between the last frost of spring and the first frost of autumn is one of the ways that we define the growing season for agriculture. It's another marker date for the diary.

10 OCTOBER | CUCKOO PINT

Remember where you found those arum leaves in the spring? Go back there and they may well have transformed into something else.

The fruit of the arum plant is a spike of bright red berries standing proudly in the hedgerow, which has given the plant a host of very rude old folk names.

These berries are poisonous and can irritate the skin, mouth and throat, but there are very few cases of serious harm.

Early arrow leaves, a strange flower and dramatic berries – this is a plant of transmutation.

11 OCTOBER | SPINDLE TREE

To say that spindle trees are nondescript is an understatement. They are a native tree that crops up sparsely in hedgerows and occasionally on a woodland edge. They have ordinary-looking leaves, tiny flowers and bark that lacks any distinctiveness, although the wood was once valued for making spinning materials and knitting needles.

Suddenly in October, the spindle leaps unexpectedly on to the dance floor with psychedelic berries in bright pink that split open to reveal bright orange seeds.

Within a week or two, the spindle will join the autumn colour parade by turning deep red, and then it will settle quietly into the background for another year.

12 OCTOBER | CONKER

Carry a conker in your pocket. Go on, don't be self-conscious. They are amazing and tactile seeds, burnished deep brown like an old dining table. There is nothing quite like carrying a bit of autumn around with you, and this will force you to go and find a tree and stamp on a spiky green seedcase in the hope of finding the perfect companion.

My memory of conkers is of having a very sore elbow: if you miss with a particularly powerful swing then the consequence is a bruising blow somewhere on your forearm. That and the sight of soft cream flesh spiralling upwards as you drill a hole through the hard case.

They remind me most of a Japanese netsuke, carved toggles with holes in that were designed to fasten a kimono. Small, smooth and highly tactile, conkers give you something to fiddle with if you are one of those people who can't keep their hands still. Who needs a netsuke when you can choose your own unique conker?

13 OCTOBER | BEECH WOOD

Take an autumn trip to the woods. My favourite at this time of year is a beech wood, a favourite of the Victorians, often planted as a feature on downs or hillsides.

An October beech wood is a wonder of tone and texture. The trees have smooth, grey, elephant-skin bark and the leaves cast such a heavy shade that barely anything grows beneath.

The leaves turn gently from green to amber and then brown, before falling to make a deep leaf litter which cloaks the woodland floor.

14 OCTOBER | WALL

I love a stone wall in autumn. The one I can see is falling down, but it is bright with moss covered in yellow-flowering stalks. The base of the wall is lined with a thatch of long grass, dotted with the odd fallen stone and the remnants of hogweed and campion.

The stones are covered with patches of white lichen and the occasional patch of black, sometimes in intersecting circles. The stones still hold the summer warmth and there are holes and cracks that offer shelter for mice, butterflies and beetles and countless more creatures.

This is the place where I saw a lizard, serpent-still then skittering, on the hottest August summer day. She is doubtless now tucked up warm for a winter sleep in among the crevices between the stones.

15 OCTOBER | HOLLOW TREE

If you haven't been inside a hollow tree then find an excuse to sneak inside while no one is looking – it's an amazing experience.

Parklands are the best place to find ancient and hollow trees. Here, large old trees have space to spread without competition for light or nutrients from surrounding youngsters.

On this day, an anniversary of the Great Storm more than 30 years ago, it is useful to notice our great hollow trees and remember why we should look after them.

Hollowness may be a sign of old age, but it doesn't mean that the tree is ill, dying or unsafe. In fact, often the opposite is true. Once a tree has reached its full height it doesn't have much use for the heartwood at the centre of its stem. All of the living tissue is around the outside, so it's a good plan to let your resident fungi eat this core in exchange for all the nutrients you need for a quiet old age.

Hollow trees can live in this state for hundreds of years and they are not even likely to fall over – during that storm of 1987 countless healthy-looking trees were felled like matchsticks while old, hollow oaks remained standing.

16 OCTOBER | LEAF COLOUR

The leaves are really starting to turn now. They are mostly still holding on tight to the trees, but shorter days and the first frosts are creating a range of leaf colours.

In New England, on the eastern seaboard of the USA, this time of year is the start of the leaf-peeping season. Our woods can certainly put on a show to match as our native trees get ready for winter.

The leaves are turning because deciduous trees no longer need the green chlorophyll to make food to grow. They start to withdraw it from the leaves while settling down for winter hibernation.

What remains is the underlying leaf colour: the yellow of field maple, dogwood red, coppery beech and all shades between. The result is a week or two of the most beautiful shades – even longer if the weather is still and the nights cold.

17 OCTOBER | NORTH STAR

It's a clear, moonlit night and it's time to get out for a winter run in the dark. It would be much easier to flop down on the sofa and turn up the fire, but I know that a blast of winter air is what I really need.

The route outwards is due north, and high up in the sky ahead of me I can see the distinctively shaped seven-star constellation of the Plough.

This is one of the easiest constellations to learn as all of the stars shine quite brightly. As the evening passes, it rotates in the northern sky and to me it looks like a wide saucepan with a kink in the handle. The two stars on the outer rim of the pan point directly towards the faint North Star.

There is no longer much need for star navigation, but it feels like a lovely thing to know nonetheless. One of my favourite stories is the escape of Shackleton's crew to South Georgia across 800 nautical miles (almost 1,500km) of ocean, guided by the brilliant star navigation of Frank Worsley.

Worsley had to rely on the stars of the Southern Hemisphere, so the Plough was not there to help him. Tonight's journey is not as dramatic; time to turn round and head southerly home.

18 OCTOBER | SHAGGY INKCAP MUSHROOM

The mown grass by the roadside is covered in lawyer's wigs.

These are shaggy inkcap mushrooms, emerging from the lush grass like a torpedo and then fanning out into broad, shaggy-scaled umbrellas with a trailing ink edge.

As with an iceberg, where nine-tenths lies below the waterline, most of the action with fungi takes place beneath the ground.

Within the soil are huge networks called mycelium, root-like threads of fungus which seek out and extract nutrients from the soil. The largest of these – quite brilliantly named the 'humongous fungus' – is a single organism that covers an area of nearly 4 sq. miles (10 sq. km) in Oregon, USA.

19 OCTOBER | ACORN

It's a mast year – the term for a bumper season of fruit from our oak trees. We are picking up handfuls of green-brown acorns from the track in the woods. They have a discoloured base where they have parted from their perfect little acorn cups.

Acorns are almost as tactile as a conker and lots of things love to eat them. The trees seem to have flooded the market in the hope that a few are trampled into the ground and survive.

Acorns were once a large part of the human diet, and in some places the right of 'pannage' – the chance to feed acorns to your pigs – was once one of the most important common rights.

20 OCTOBER | LOMBARDY POPLAR

We have many fewer orchards than we used to and perhaps many fewer Lombardy poplars as a result.

They were once planted as shelter trees for orchards and they grow exceptionally fast – 6ft (1.8m) or more in a season.

Like the other poplar trees, the white poplar and our very scarce black poplar, they are probably not a tree to plant in your garden. They throw out hundreds of suckers from their roots and spread wildly. In America they are called cottonwood trees because of their wind-blown seeds.

Like sheep, they look best at a distance. A few marking a hill-top conjure images of cypresses in Tuscany as they stand tall and slim on the horizon.

21 OCTOBER | APPLE DAY

Pick an apple from the tree. They don't appear to have psychedelic qualities, but nothing takes you through the looking glass of nature faster than eating a crunchy English apple.

It is our humble fruit, resident of lunch boxes and filler of crumbles. At this time of year you can celebrate 'apple day', which gives you the chance to taste dozens of different types of apples. You can crush some fresh juice or even, like me, attempt the manufacture of questionable cider.

Yet, the domestic apple hails, it is thought, not from an English orchard or hedgerow, but from high up in the fruit forests of the Tian Shan mountains of China and Kyrgyzstan and Kazakhstan.

It turns out that we can enjoy sweet apples because brown bears have a sweet tooth too: over the course of thousands of years, choosy bears favoured the trees with the sweetest apples. An apple seed eaten by a bear passes straight through its gut and has a good chance of germinating.

At some point in the distant past, people discovered these apples high up in the western fringe of the Himalayas and transported them all over the world. They now play a big role in many cultures.

22 OCTOBER | LAPWING

It's one of those stormy days with a cold north-westerly wind that is trundling heavy showers across the plain towards us.

In between the rain, the low sun turns the sky a deep purple-grey. Against this dark backdrop comes a sudden flash of white. There it is again – lapwings, a flock of them, swinging in unison against the flint breeze.

In winter lapwings, with their long crests on their heads and their smart, iridescent feathers, gather together on farmland and marsh.

These birds, more commonly called the peewit after their call, are waders that have moved into our fields. They were once commonplace in the landscape. Now, a flock of lapwings is something to hope for over a ploughed field on a chill winter's day.

23 OCTOBER | DEER RUT

It is time to roar like a stag: the deer rut is in full swing.

Bolving is the sport of roaring like a deer, in the hope of receiving an answer from a stag. On the Eastern Moors above Sheffield, it is an annual contest, with points awarded for volume, authenticity and every stag reply.

The deer rut is the process by which the pecking order of a deer herd is established, with the dominant males earning the right to mate with the females. It's a time of year to give deer a wide berth as the males are spoiling for a fight.

The deer rut happens in our parklands too. Here the fallow deer also live in large herds and the start of autumn is the season for noisy displays, posturing and rutting.

24 OCTOBER | DECOMPOSITION

A big October storm has scattered leaves beneath the trees, forming little piles against the exposed roots.

It's time to tip your cap to nature's tidying-up brigade: the decomposers. Like it or not, everything in nature is anchored to the circle of life. It is the decomposers that join up the bottom of the circle.

The fallen leaves are a chance to get to work. On a lawn you can sometimes see a leaf poking vertically into the grass where an earthworm is busy tugging it below the surface. Turn over a heap of leaves after a few days and it will be full of woodlice and millipedes and the tiny little larvae of gnats and flies.

The fungi are at work too. In an old leaf pile you may find the thin, white fungal hyphae strung between the leaves. There are slime moulds at work too. Within a year the leaves will have become part of the woodland floor – a dark, rich leaf mould, full of goodness to power a burst of new growth each spring.

25 OCTOBER | SCOTS PINE

Lots of our conifer trees have been introduced from elsewhere, but the Scots pine is one of only three native conifers (along with the juniper and yew).

It was once widespread, colonising from Europe after the last Ice Age, and in Scotland ancient trees survive as fragments of the great Caledonian Forest.

When oak was used to build naval ships, Scots pine provided the timber for the masts and spars – tall, straight and flexible – and the resin to caulk the planks.

Pine trees are hard to tell apart, but if you see one beside a field or in a churchyard then a guess of 'Scots pine' is usually a good bet.

26 OCTOBER | PHEASANT

Pheasants are so commonplace in some parts of the country that it is hard to imagine that they are only here to be shot. Each year nearly 40 million pheasants are released into the landscape. The first pheasants were introduced nearly a thousand years ago from the mountains of Georgia, but the more common varieties now hail from western China.

Put aside your thoughts on shooting for a moment and appreciate the pheasant. They are incredibly handsome birds and when they fly off they often leave you a present of one of their great long barred tail feathers that you can put in your hat – if you have one.

27 OCTOBER | WINTER FIELD

It is time for a long walk along the footpath beside huge ploughed fields.

Once the fields would have lain bare all winter with a short stubble beard, ready for ploughing in the spring. Now the seed drill usually follows the harvester and so the field is already covered with the soft green covering of next year's crop.

This is one of those lovely fields with a large, wide flower margin and there are a few still blooming despite the frost. Field speedwell trails pale blue among the young crops and the groundsel still bears a yellow bloom or two among the seedheads.

Jackdaws float in lazy packs in the distance and the occasional pheasant squawk shatters the silence.

28 OCTOBER | SUCCESSION

The leaves have fallen now and you can start to pick up the structure of the landscape more clearly.

The hills above the town are cloaked in woodland which creates a timeless scene. Yet it's not timeless at all. On the old maps and photographs much of this hill was crew-cut-short, sheep-grazing country and the Bronze Age burial mound at the top commanded views across the vale.

Imperceptibly, the hawthorn has spread from the hedgerows to create scrubby woodland, which in turn is slowly being overtopped by sycamore, oak and maple. This is the process of succession, which in most cases leads to fields 'tumbling down to woodland'.

Yet, we now think that the ancient landscape was shaped by another strong force as well. Succession pushes one way and grazing pushes the other. Not too far back into history these woods were filled with big grazing animals: elk, an ancient cow called an aurochs, ponies, wild boar and deer that would have created large, open areas. Maybe the burial mound always commanded a terrific view.

29 OCTOBER | LONDON PLANE

Plane trees have the best bark of any tree there is. That's it, no discussion needed. It flakes into a pattern like sand and mud at the base of a dried-up lake.

These hybrid trees are tough as old boots and they line streets with maple-like leaves and statuesque stems. If a nightingale ever did sing in Berkeley Square, it was most likely from one of the tallest plane trees.

They are a mixture of the American and Oriental plane and they were probably imported from Spain in the seventeenth century. The oldest of the London planes, at Barn Elms in south-west London, dates from the 1680s.

They also pepper Lancelot 'Capability' Brown landscapes like a signature – stop to admire a view and you may well find yourself beneath an ancient plane, planted there by the genius landscape-maker himself.

30 OCTOBER | FUNGI NAMES

For the last 15 years or so the experts at the British Mycological Society have had a special working party to select English names for some of the 15,000 fungi that are found in the UK.

The strictly written protocol notes that 'word play has also been possible on occasion and provides one of the best means of reflecting British culture'.

No kidding. Look at this selection …

Pavement mushroom · bearded fieldcap · pink disco · snakeskin grisette · false deathcap · destroying angel · upper crust · club foot · hair sedge smut · purple jellydisc · powdery piggyback · barometer earthstar · the pretender · the humpback · dewdrop dapperling · golden navel · devil's fingers · mealy frosted funnel · lentil shanklet · tiger's eye · distinguished inkcap · bug sputnik · cinnamon jellybaby · King Alfred's cakes · snaketongue truffleclub · funeral bell · twisted deceiver · chicken of the woods · bald knight · cryptic bonnet · vampires bane · hotlips · Jack O'lantern · bonfire cauliflower · the flirt · powdercap strangler · plums and custard

31 OCTOBER | HALLOWE'EN

I love the fact that our culture is a bit of a hodgepodge. This time of year is one of the best examples.

People in parts of these islands used to mark this night as the Celtic festival of Samhain, the night where the boundaries between the living and the dead became blurred. The invading Romans brought us two festivals that happened around this time of year, including the tradition of honouring Pomona, the fruit goddess.

The Christians rebranded this night All Hallows' Eve, which, to be honest, sounds a lot less fun.

Nonetheless, nineteenth-century English and Irish emigrants took the idea to the USA and they have now exported it back to us, with added pumpkins.

Whichever way you spin it, all of this partying is really about the turning of the year. It is the end of harvest and the beginning of the dark months. A time to dress up like a Celt, bob apples like a Roman and eat pumpkin pie like a true American.

NOVEMBER

Everything closes in. This is the season to hunker down and embrace the dark.

It feels like an ending of things. The last of the leaves fall, water sloughs off sodden fields. Yet there are beginnings, too. Tawny owls hoot from the conifer trees and newly arrived redwings whistle in the hedgerows.

Lakes and wetlands are alive with the sharp calls of coots and chatter-quack of ducks. It is time to walk among trees on soft heaven-cloths of amber and gold, where white mushrooms light the woodland floor beyond.

Left: Silver birch trees.

1 NOVEMBER | QUARTER DAY

Hallowe'en marks the end of harvest season. Today, sometimes called All Saints' Day, is the start of the dark months, and in many cultures it is a special day.

There are six weeks until the year turns again. It's time for a bonfire, lots of lights and a party. It is no accident that this time of year is full of festivals of light and fire – Diwali and Hanukkah as well as Samhain.

It's an in-between time. For me, it is the day to resolve to spend the next six weeks enjoying candlelight, friendship and fires, while spending every possible daylight minute outside enjoying the sudden sparseness of the landscape and the soft light of winter.

2 NOVEMBER | ASH KEY

High up in the leafless ash trees hang bunches of ash keys: the tree produces a prolific number of seeds, each shaped like half a sycamore seed with a similar ability to spiral on the breeze.

Ash trees are one of the defining trees of our landscape. You can recognise them from their black, ash-dipped buds on stems that turn upwards at the end.

Ash wood is used to make cricket stumps and provides the best winter firewood. Passing a sick child through a split ash tree was a traditional way of curing disease. They are the tree of life.

Yet, our poor ash trees are dying fast – victims of a new disease called ash dieback that seems to strike at groups of ash at a time. I can't quite believe that ash will go the same way as the big elms I remember from childhood, which used to be the starling roost in the fields beyond our houses.

The ash keys carry hope. The ability to grow from seed so readily means that ash trees are a diverse bunch, and perhaps some of them will be sufficiently resistant to allow them to survive.

In some cultures this is the Day of the Dead. Today I am crossing all of my fingers hoping for a resurrection.

3 NOVEMBER | HIBERNATION

Hibernation is a great tactic to survive in a cold climate. I am sometimes tempted to take up the practice myself.

If you are a bear then this is the time of year to settle down for a winter sleep. In the UK, only dormice, hedgehogs and bats really hibernate, and they are just about settling down now.

Over the winter animals slow their bodies down into a state of torpor and rely on fat stores built up over the autumn to tide them through until spring.

Bees seal themselves up in hollow stems or bury themselves in the ground. Butterflies such as peacocks seek out the corner of a shed for a winter sleep. Some insects go one step further into a state of suspended animation called diapause.

This year, I am not going to wish for the ability to hibernate. I am going to learn to love November.

 BIRD'S NEST

The hedgerows have been cut and now is a fantastic time to look for birds' nests. They are no longer in use, but it is a great way of beginning to understand how birds think.

It takes a while to get your eye in, but if you can find a long stretch of a nice high hedge then you may find several nests. The deeper and thicker the hedge, the better a place it is to nest – somewhere too thick and thorny for marauding magpies and squirrels is ideal.

At the top of the hedge you may find a wood pigeon's nest – usually a poorly assembled affair made of loose twigs. Where the hedge has been cut, chaffinches or blackbirds use the forks in the branches as a base for a neat, circular home.

I like to look out for the nests of long-tailed tits, beautifully constructed globes of moss and spiders' webs with an entry hole at the side.

5 NOVEMBER | BONFIRE

Thor, the Norse weather god, had a favourite month. It was, of course, November, season of darkness, storms and thunder.

The early November celebrations here are about bonfire night. This is the season for tidying up all the growth from last year after all – although let's not get too tidy about it, as we need to leave some spaces for all those things that hibernate in and under dead vegetation. Top of my list to look out for are the hedgehogs that might have snuck into the bonfire pile, as I don't want to accidentally burn any of them.

I shan't be burning any effigies on my bonfire either – I want no part of attempts to hijack some ancient rituals with some recent religious tribalism about plots and Guys.

6 NOVEMBER | BRACKET FUNGUS

The birch tree has a ladder of bracket fungus growing on it. I think this one is a horse's hoof fungus, with a grey-black, hard surface.

You can easily pass them by, but we know for sure that our ancestors would not have done so. A horse's hoof fungus could be the difference between life and death.

In 1991, the body of a 5,300-year-old Neolithic man nicknamed Ötzi the Iceman was found in a glacier on the border between Austria and Italy. In among his few possessions was a leather bag containing fragments of this special bracket fungus.

Horse's hoof fungus is one of the best types of tinder: it burns even from a cool flint spark. If you can make fire, then you can survive.

There are lots of bracket fungi, many of which live for years and grow into huge, semi-circular 'conks'. You may not need to carry tinder with you, but make like your ancestors nonetheless and give them a nod as you pass.

7 NOVEMBER | FIELDFARE

The autumn migration is not just something for swans and geese. Suddenly the hedgerows and fields contain flocks of birds. Walk along a narrow lane and birds peel off ahead of you with a clattering call. The fieldfares have arrived.

Fieldfares are big thrushes – slightly bigger than a blackbird, but a mix of grey, brown and white with a spotted breast. They are here to escape European snow and gorge on hedgerow berries.

They are a moustachioed sergeant major of a bird. Leave out an apple or two and you may get a close look as they strut about.

8 NOVEMBER | REDWING

In among the fieldfares there will be redwings too. They are easy to mistake for a song thrush, but have a pronounced eyebrow and a flash of red beneath each wing.

They are a little smaller than fieldfares and have a soft whistle rather than a chattering call.

When the weather gets really cold, redwings will turn up in gardens and parks, hunting for any berries that they can find.

They will be here until the spring before heading back off to the far north to breed on the fringes of the northern pine forests of Norway or the lava fields of Iceland.

9 NOVEMBER | HAW BERRY

The white flowers of the hawthorn in May have given way to crimson haw berries that also cloak the outgrown hedges.

These autumn fruits are rich in vitamin C and would once have been boiled down into a leathery fruit treat for the winter. Some people still make jam out of them, too.

This is what our redwings and fieldfares have travelled all this way for: a sweet, autumnal feast. It's a really good reason to cut hedges sparingly, or one year in three, rather than be too fierce with the flail.

10 NOVEMBER | FROZEN POND

'Earth stood hard as iron, water like a stone'. ('In the Bleak Midwinter', Christina Rossetti, 1906.) It is much too early for carols, but no one has told the weather. The puddles have frozen solid, with the ice forming concentric steps towards the centre of each puddle as the frost has followed the falling water level.

The ponds are frozen too, and so it's time to put a little warm water out for the birds. As long as the pond doesn't freeze completely, much of the wildlife can adapt just fine. The frogs will bury themselves in the mud, become dormant and breathe through their skin.

The real pond specialists, diving beetles and water boatmen, mooch about hunting for air bubbles beneath the ice. Other larvae have long since crawled out to overwinter in the dead vegetation beside the water.

11 NOVEMBER | CHURCHYARD

It's a day for remembering; time for a nature walk through the churchyard.

These little treasured patches of ground are full of wildlife. The inevitable yew trees provide places for shelter and berries for bird food. Other evergreens and ivy mean that even in the depths of winter your arrival is greeted by the call of a robin, a willow tit or a wren.

The grass is left longer and mown less often. Aside from human contributions to the circle of life, there should be no need for fertiliser here. Some of the old stones are sinking softly into the hallowed turf.

For the last couple of years, ravens have started to nest high up in the cedar trees and disrupted the scene with their harsh croaking. They are gone now and all is at peace. Pause awhile and listen.

12 NOVEMBER | BUZZARD

There is something circling above me that looks just like an eagle, calling across the valley like a mewing cat, with a squat tail and wings that are 4ft (1.2m) wide.

This is a buzzard – the comeback kid. This eagle-like hawk has returned to our lowland landscape.

They like woodland to nest in, building huge, scruffy nests at the top of the taller trees. They vary wildly in colour from deep brown all over to a pale cream. They are opportunists, eating the roadkill of voles and rabbits, or insects and earthworms when prey is in short supply.

Fifty years ago this would have been a rare sight, due to the presence of the pesticide DDT in the food chain and persecution. Not any more – now everyone can see a buzzard on the edge of town, flying circles in the winter sky.

13 NOVEMBER | IVY FLOWER

Our Gothic, evergreen, rambling ivy has another trick up its sleeve – the late arrival of a host of creamy, pollen-clad flowers.

Flowering ivy is very valuable at this time of year. There are few other sources of nectar, so any insect brave enough to be out and about makes a beeline for the ivy flowers on any sunny wall.

Ivy is one of those evergreens that hints at immortality and has long been associated with magical powers. In winter, an ivy-wrapped tree is a sheltering space for all kinds of creatures. It seems to defy the dying back of autumn by becoming brighter and greener.

Next month, when the flowers have given way to clusters of black berries, it will be time to cut some ivy to bring into the house for the turning of the year. For now though, let's leave it for the bees.

14 NOVEMBER | HOGWEED STEM

Unlike the cow parsley, the hogweed stems last the winter through.

If you get up early enough they are dressed by the frost like the return of the flowers that graced these bee-dazing plants in June.

Leave them where you find them all winter. Not only do they have a great architectural quality, but the hollow stems are also a fantastic hatching place for next year's wave of insects.

A hollow hogweed stem is a popular winter hibernation spot for all the lacewings and ladybirds that will keep the aphids in check in the spring.

15 NOVEMBER | ROOK

The rooks are clustered in the field like a sombre band of gravediggers.

They have a bare patch of greyish skin at the base of their beaks – perhaps because they spend a lot of time beak-deep in the soft earth.

Rooks are particularly fond of leatherjackets – the larvae of the cranefly – and their enthusiasm means that lawns, fields and golf courses look like they have been attacked with spears.

If the rooks don't eat them then the larvae will kill the grass anyway in the spring – making them the curse of groundsmen everywhere. As a cricketer, I have to digress to share the fact that, in 1935, a wonderfully named South African cricketer called Xenophon Constantine Balaskas bowled his side to a first overseas Test victory on what was described by *Wisden* as a 'leatherjacket-ravaged pitch' at Lords.

There is really nothing sombre about a rook save their funereal garb. They are clever, sociable birds and I am fond of them, whereas I can't quite warm to their cousin, the carrion crow, a fiercer, more solitary stalker.

16 NOVEMBER | WAXCAP MUSHROOM

This is the time of year for finding jewels among the grass. Waxcap mushrooms appear suddenly overnight, and old lawns, churchyards and parks all play host to them.

They seem to like old, low, mossy grass and they are a sign of grassland free from the curse of fertiliser. If you have waxcaps, you will have other fungi and wild flowers too.

Waxcaps live up to their name: they are shaped as a mushroom should be, with a shiny, waxed top that comes in a fantastic range of colours. They bring some gentle excitement to a walk in late November.

The yellow waxcap is the most common, but you may find green, red, white or brown varieties as well. There is also a single pink variety – the ballerina waxcap – which is rare but a real speciality of these islands. That's something to hope for on a dank late autumn day.

MOORHEN

Don't take your neighbouring moorhen for granted. If you have ever fed the ducks then you will have seen a moorhen, even if you didn't know its name. You will recognise their characteristic squawk as well.

They really should be called a marsh-hen, rather than a moorhen. They are year-round residents of any stream, lake or pond, not a creature of moorland.

The moorhen is a stay-at-home kind of bird. Arctic terns may migrate from pole to pole, but moorhens seem quite happy with the lake where they grew up, thank you very much. It takes all sorts.

They are handsome birds with red beaks with a yellow tip, and smart feathers in black, purple and brown. In the water they seem entirely in proportion, but if you see one on land you would be forgiven for thinking that it had borrowed a pair of feet from a bird twice its size.

18 NOVEMBER | COOT

Coots and moorhens go together. They are the two ever-present birds of a winter lake.

Like a moorhen, they are sleek in the water and comical on land. They are black with a striking white flash above their beak that gives them the appearance of a receding hairline – perhaps this is why we use the expression 'bald as a coot'.

Moorhens tend to potter around the edges of a lake, or up on the side of the bank, whereas coots seem happier gliding on open water.

19 NOVEMBER | MIST

Gilbert White: 'November 19, 1776 – This afternoon the weather turning suddenly very warm produced an unusual appearance; for the dew on the windows was on the outside of the glass, the air being warmer abroad than within.'

It is not all cold and grey in November. There is still a ghost of heat in the low sun, and when the wind turns south, there is a hint of fading summer. Late insects venture out and catch the light.

Warmth brings mist, which lies low over the ground as the evening draws in. In the low light, the furrows of the old farming systems fill with a soft, grey haze.

It may be a brief respite, but any hint of November warmth is an excuse to sit outside with a warm cup in your hand.

20 NOVEMBER | MUNTJAC BARK

The quiet darkness is shattered by a single bark. A few seconds of silence and then another; actually it is somewhere between a bark and a shriek.

It's not a dog or even a fox, but one of the deer family – a muntjac – and spooky, metronomic barking is one of the things that they do.

Muntjacs are another Chinese animal that has made their home here, and they are really successful. They were only introduced to Woburn in Bedfordshire in the early twentieth century and have now spread far and wide.

You are more likely to hear than see one, but if you do catch sight of a muntjac they don't really look like a deer at all. They are hunched like a hyena, with small, swept-back antlers and a distinctive striped face.

21 NOVEMBER | GROUNDSEL

Groundsel is a proper weed, a coverer of bare ground and an occupier of field edges. It is a highly adaptable plant, resistant to some sprays and tolerant of salt and pollution.

It has yellow, tube-like flowers, which don't appear to have petals; these are then followed by a tuft of seeds like an old man's grey hair.

Don't dismiss it too quickly. Anything that flowers in November deserves a bit of attention. This is a cousin of the ragwort flower and it also provides food for those beautiful little cinnabar moths that you may have seen in the summer. No? Well there is always next year.

22 NOVEMBER | FOX

Last year, a quiet winter supper at a friend's house in town was interrupted by a visit from the wild: a fox, skulking then stock-still, gazing through the window with a quizzical look.

November is the mating season for foxes and they are out and about looking for a partner. They fill the night air with screams and yelps.

It is also the season of the 'fox fires': the Finnish name for the northern lights that light winter evenings at high latitudes. Our skies are too light to see them now, but it was not always thus. Gilbert White's diary from this day in 1777 notes 'Strong N. aurora, extending to the W and SW, some streaks of fiery red.'

The Finnish story is that the auroras were created by foxes running over the crystal-glass snow, throwing sparks in their wake. How I would love to see the northern lights from my window reflected in a sharp winter snow! Never mind, I shall have to make do with a fox sighting: perhaps slinking through the sodden morning grass or jumping into a night-time hedgerow.

23 NOVEMBER | BEECH NUT

Beneath the beech trees lies a carpet of broken seedcases. Split into three, the beech nut pods have a rough, hairy outer and the softest, pale brown interior.

If you can find one that is unopened then you can gently prise the three parts of the case apart to reveal the beautiful, triangular, nut-brown seeds.

Like acorns, beech nuts are an ancient food, although they need to be roasted or treated first. Around here, they seem to be the favoured snack for the squirrels.

24 NOVEMBER | ORION

The three evenly spaced stars of Orion's belt have crept over the southern horizon and have taken up their rightful place in the winter sky.

This is one of the easiest constellations to recognise and it will be around until the spring: Orion the hunter. His dog Sirius has a star named for him too – lying low but bright in the southern sky.

Orion is one of those constellations in which stars are still being made. The cloudy Orion nebula is a cluster of young stars, spinning outwards to fill our galaxy with light.

So, if it has been a long day, take a moment for a quick glance at Orion. It is a reminder that we are all made from nothing but the dust of stars.

25 NOVEMBER | SILVER BIRCH

There is a painting by Gustav Klimt that captures an autumn birch wood perfectly: a scene of orange, diamond-shaped leaves framed by delicate white stems.

Austere, stark, shining in any hint of sunlight, birch is the archetypal winter tree. It shrugs off snow with flexible, broom-twig branches and bends to bear the toughest of winds.

Birch is a coloniser tree – on poor soils it fills any gap with a thousand seedlings – first mover and edge filler.

They are at their best in winter: trees of the far north that look most at home when the weather turns cold.

26 NOVEMBER

TEASEL STEM

The teasel stems of summer have lost their spiralling pink flowers. The hum of bees is a memory. Yet they still stand, brown and sere, marking the forgotten corner that they colonised in the spring.

With no other vegetation around, you can now see that they are absolutely covered in tiny little thorns. Just like the hogweed, these tall stems make a great insect hiding place.

Each seedhead holds a couple of thousand seeds. While the bees have long gone, you may instead be greeted by a charming goldfinch chatter and a flash of yellow wings as you approach.

27 NOVEMBER | YARROW

Yarrow is a flower of demigods, a wondrous healing herb used on the war-torn plains below the walls of Troy. It also flowers on the verge outside my local supermarket – even in late November.

There is almost a whole book to be written about 'plants that look a bit like cow parsley'. Yarrow is one of these, although once you look closely it is clear that it comes from a different family entirely.

It has white clusters of flowers and dark green, feathery leaves, and is the plant described in Homer's *Iliad* as 'the bitter herb'. Its Latin name, *Achillea millefolium*, honours Achilles, warrior and healer of Greek mythology, who taught his men to use the plant to staunch wounds on the battlefield.

It is also known as the milfoil, or 'thousand leaf', and its medicinal qualities are supported by science as well as myth. For me, the quality of flowering in November is just as much of a quality to be treasured.

28 NOVEMBER | OLD MAN'S BEARD

You might think of clematis as an exotic summer garden plant, trained up a pergola perhaps, with bright purple flowers.

Yet we have a native clematis as well. It has the nickname traveller's joy, and at this flowerless time of year you can see why: hedges, banks and walls are adorned with silver, feathery seedheads.

It's also called old man's beard, and one look at the glorious, architectural scrambling of the stems explains why. It is one of those plants that looks like it is going to take over the whole landscape. In young woodland it can climb high up the trees creating Tarzan-ready stems that can be as thick as your forearm.

The finches will be at the seeds before too long, so now is a time to enjoy them at their height.

29 NOVEMBER | HEDGE PLANTING

It is the start of the tree-planting season. If it has been very mild then you might even want to wait until December.

Our deciduous trees are dormant in winter, and this is the time to lift them out of the ground and move them.

If you can, it is even better to let trees grow on their own as they tend to get away much faster from seed.

However, I have a hedge to plant, and that requires a bit more work. Many of the hedges that define our landscape were planted after enclosure – dominated by blackthorn and hawthorn. If you are planting a hedge yourself then you can mix it up a bit more – we have some fantastic shrubs that make brilliant hedges and don't mind being cut back hard to thicken them.

30 NOVEMBER | TREE WORDS

It is National Tree Week, a time to honour and cherish our long-lived friends who make the whole world more three-dimensional.

Sat in the woods after felling some trees for firewood (woods need to be managed too), I look around with a mental note of the families of our native British trees.

Alder · ash · aspen · beech · birch · blackthorn · box · buckthorn · cherry · crab apple · dogwood · elder · elm · hawthorn · hazel · holly · hornbeam · juniper · lime · maple · oak · poplar · rowan · Scots pine · spindle · whitebeam · wild service tree · willow · yew

DECEMBER

There are three short weeks until the solstice and the return of the light.

It is time to celebrate the turning of the year by filling the house with magical evergreens, holly branches and pine cones.

It's the season to walk outside on a frosty evening listening for an animal screech in the dark.

Birds come close in search of food and water. Gangs of jackdaws and finch flocks roam in the winter gusts.

Left: Goldfinches and a greenfinch on burdock.

1 DECEMBER | MOTHS

Unlike our butterflies, the hardy moths mark the whole year round. I started the year with a winter moth and can end it with a December moth.

For me, the big day-flying moths – the oak eggar and garden tiger – were the childhood moths of summer. Bringing up a caterpillar and watching it transform into a moth remains one of the most amazing nature experiences, and it is something I wish every child could do.

December moths are related to oak eggar moths, although they are much smaller – about 1in (2.5cm). They have charcoal grey-brown wings with creamy white markings in a wave pattern.

These moths are night-flying moths, but if you have an outside light they may well pay you a December visit.

2 DECEMBER | STARLING MURMURATION

I am sitting, shivering, overlooking the river sunset and hoping for something miraculous.

In winter starlings gather together in giant flocks. As darkness falls they come together to create a shifting, folding shape in the sky. This is a murmuration and you may see one anywhere starlings like to roost – near a pier, in town or over a reed-bed.

At a distance the murmuration looks like smoke twisting in the breeze. It whirls, pulses and falls as if the birds are a single sheet of black silk being waved and folded by an invisible hand.

It would be easy to believe that magic is at work. Yet, just like a sunflower and a pine cone, the laws of nature – simple rules and complex patterns – are at work again.

It turns out that each starling simply watches the seven or so birds around it and tries to follow each change of direction. That is all that is needed to create a mirage sufficient to fool a marauding peregrine or sparrowhawk.

3 DECEMBER | TREE BARK

The sycamore tree has a crackled surface of shards of bark, as if the growth of the tree has forced an arboreal impersonation of the shirt of the Incredible Hulk.

It is customary to be rude about the sycamore as it does not support nearly as many specialist insects as other trees (perhaps slightly more than a dozen). Yet it is a winter shelter to a whole range of creatures: ladybirds, lacewings, millipedes and more.

Beneath this bark flake is a rabble of earwigs. They gather in clusters under the bark and look very cross to be disturbed, waving their pincers at me in disgust before scuttling away further into the scales of the tree.

4 DECEMBER | TAWNY OWL

'December 4, 1770 – Most owls seem to hoot exactly in B flat according to several pitch-pipes used in tuning of harpsichords, & sold as strictly at concert pitch.'

Tonight I am playing the piano to an owl. Every time I hear a hoot I am giving them a long B flat note in response.

The hoot in question is the sound of a big tawny owl. They are noisy in December as they are getting together to breed – they are one of the earliest birds to lay eggs in the late winter.

Everyone knows that owls say 'too-whit, too-whoo'. Not everyone knows that this sound is the work of *two* owls! The lady says 'too-whit' and the man responds 'too-whoo'. It's an owl love duet.

If you can impersonate an owl then they will sometimes answer you back. They are territorial so you may get more than you bargained for as they come to take a closer look.

It was Gilbert White's brother Henry who noticed that owls sing in B flat (I will be able to vouch for this when I get an answer to my piano). Apparently he wandered around the village with a set of pan pipes as part of his research, which is an image that warms my heart.

Tawny owls are not our only owls, but they are much the commonest and most widespread. I dare you to hoot back ...

5 DECEMBER | GREAT CRESTED GREBE

Winter lakes do not just have mallards, coots and moorhens. Even in town, a lake may also play home to the exotic great crested grebe. They look a little more ordinary in winter, but in their summer plumage they are dramatic birds with a tuft of feathers and an orange neck.

Once you have found a place with grebes then you must make a diary note for early spring to come back and hope to see their mating dance. The birds seem almost to stand upon the water, with their crested heads fanned out in a plume conducting a mirror-image dance.

There is no such excitement in December.

6 DECEMBER | LOG PILE

Today I am going to make a home for longhorn beetles. I am even hoping for a stag beetle, although that may be in vain. What these creatures need is a pile of dead wood. Decaying timber is incredibly valuable for wildlife and there isn't enough of it about. We have all got too tidy.

So, today is a good day to make a log pile. I have found a shady spot and I am digging into the soil so that the first layer of logs settles into the earth. Some leftover hazel and an old tree stump will do the job.

Log piles provide a home for all the specialist insects that feed on decaying wood, including my longhorn beetles. The wood is consumed by fungi (which in turn gives more insects a place to live). In time ferns and mosses will colonise a log pile and they make brilliant hibernation places for mice, voles, frogs and toads.

7 DECEMBER | BURDOCK SEED

I have returned from a December walk with big round burrs attached to my socks. The dog has the same problem and is doing contortions to try to chew them out of her fur.

These are burdock seeds that have detached from dead stems that are still standing. In 1941 the same thing happened to the Swiss engineer George de Mestral while he was hunting in the Jura mountains in Switzerland.

Rather than complain about the inconvenience, he put the seeds under a microscope, and seven years later he patented a new fastener called Velcro, with a name based on the French words for velvet ('velour') and hook ('crochet').

Once you have extracted the seeds from sock or pet, look at them closely and you will see exactly the source of George's inspiration.

8 DECEMBER | KING ALFRED'S CAKE

The dead branches of the ash trees are covered in little black cakes.

King Alfred may have united England, founded the Navy and promoted universal education, but he is equally famous for his questionable culinary skills. King Alfred's cakes are a common fungus found throughout Britain and Ireland. If you pick one and cut it you can see silvery concentric rings, each one representing a year of growth. They are another smouldering tinder fungus that was once valued as a source of fire.

I like to think of Alfred scattering his burnt cakes through the forest whenever I see them.

9 DECEMBER | MOON HALO

'Ring around the moon makes rain soon.'

It's one of those crisp, frosty nights and theie is a halo around the moon. There may indeed be rain on the way – high clouds are streaming in from the west, tens of thousands of feet overhead.

The ice crystals in the high clouds are refracting the light into a 22-degree halo, always the same distance whatever the conditions. It is a circular white rainbow in the sky, and it is unique to your viewpoint – everyone sees the moon through a different set of ice crystals.

10 DECEMBER | HORNBEAM

The hedge around the garden is hung with dead brown leaves that clatter in the wind. The tree looks a little like beech and makes a similar hedge, but the leaves have toothed edges and parallel ridges that set them apart.

Hornbeams are trees, not shrubs; you have to keep cutting them to make a hedge. They have very hard (horn-like) wood that burns hot. In Hainault Forest in Essex, there are hundreds of ancient hornbeam trees, which once were cut as pollards every few years to provide bundles of fuel for the bakeries of east London.

When London burned in 1666, it was quite probably started by the fuel of the hornbeam tree.

They make a brilliant hedge, although it is a shame to cut them really. A pollarded hornbeam with metallic bark and twisted, spreading branches is a wonderful sight.

11 DECEMBER

SWEET CHESTNUT

It's the season to roast chestnuts on an open fire – or to grab some from a brazier while doing your Christmas shopping.

Chestnuts are the fruit of vigorous trees that love a sandy soil. They have big saw-toothed leaves and trunks with twisted bark. The fruit have become part of our Christmas and the trees part of our landscape, producing fabulous split poles for fencing and the original posts for supporting hops.

At Croft Castle in the hop country of Herefordshire there is an ancient sweet chestnut avenue that is reputed to have grown from chestnuts found in one of the ships from the Spanish Armada (a great story, but the trees are probably 80 years younger than that).

Eating a Christmas chestnut instantly conjures a bright September day at Croft when the trees along the avenue were covered with green, sea-urchin chestnut cases, fiercely spiked and each containing burnished nuts within.

12 DECEMBER | PINE CONE

The Scots pine trees in the churchyard around the corner are offering an early Christmas gift. It is time to go and gather a few pine cones.

The cedars alongside them drop cones of a different shape, circular and tightly packed.

Pine cones are an adaptation that protect the seeds from hungry birds, frost and fire. The scales on a cone spiral around them and stay clamped shut until the weather warms.

The cones can stay on the tree for years, but in late autumn some will break loose and fall to the ground – just in time for Christmas decorations.

13 DECEMBER | MARS – AND METEORS

Tonight is a night to put on your warmest coat and take a friend to watch the night sky. Mars often shines brighter than all the stars in the southern sky at this time of year. Even if you can't get a good view of the stars, you have a good chance of seeing Mars on a winter evening.

A glimpse of the red planet is amazing enough, but tonight is one of the best meteor nights of the year, so it is time to turn your gaze to the sky.

The Geminids meteors are another set of asteroid fragments that arrive at this time of year as a shower of shooting stars. Look up at the south-western sky and get ready to make a wish.

14 DECEMBER | ROE DEER PRINT

There is a cloven hoofprint on the path through the woods and the wall is broken down where something has been crossing. The bark of a young sycamore has been shredded at chest height.

These are the marks of a roe deer. My tracking skills are not brilliant, but I can be fairly certain about this because roe deer are real creatures of habit and I have seen them lurking at the edge of the wood as I travel past in the mornings.

Despite the fact that there are half a million roe deer in the UK, a sighting is rare and magical. They are pretty deer, with a black nose and a white flash on their rear. The bucks have a neat pair of small antlers.

Robert Graves, the poet and author, described the roebuck as 'the keeper of the secret' – the mythical and fleeting deer of legend.

That is how I feel about them too.

15 DECEMBER | POLYPODY FERN

As the other plants die away, the ferns come to the fore. The trees by the river are clad in polypody ferns, growing without any soil, using the trees as anchor points.

It's time for a quick fern recap. The big buckler ferns are still around, accompanied by their cousins the male ferns and lady ferns. The hartstongue ferns that unfurled in spring are still visible too – darker and more ragged than before. In contrast, the bracken has long since died back to a thatch of brown fronds.

There are three species of polypody, and all look similar, a little like a ladder with fronds made up of simple, finger-like leaflets growing out from the main stem. On the back of each leaf are clusters of yellow and orange dots that carry spores which will provide the next generation of ferns.

16 DECEMBER | HOLLY

Today is the day to bring some nature into the house. This week I get the urge to fill the house with evergreens: holly and ivy for wreaths, a Christmas tree and some mistletoe under which to kiss.

Once a branch of holly would have been used to decorate houses rather than a Christmas tree. Holly is one of our native evergreen trees with beautiful, waxy leaves and red berries.

We think of holly leaves as being fiercely prickly, but if you look at a young holly leaf then it has few, if any, prickles and trees were once cut to provide winter feed for cattle and sheep. A winter feed of holly is a good way to cheer up the animals – like a winter vitamin shot.

The prickly leaves had male associations, while the smooth leaves were female, and it was said that whichever was on the branch that was cut for Christmas would determine whether the husband or wife would rule the household for the rest of the year.

I know which branch I shall be cutting. There is no point fighting it.

17 DECEMBER | NORWAY SPRUCE

The annual trip to the sawmill to fetch a Christmas tree is something that has become as much a family tradition as the dressing of the tree.

The ancient pagan tradition of gathering holly branches has been replaced by the European habit of bringing in a conifer tree – originally the Norway spruce, a tree that forms forests right up to the fringes of the Arctic.

I think that we have Prince Albert to blame for the spruce tree, although spruce itself has some ancient associations: the Greeks believed it was the tree of Artemis, goddess of the moon.

18 DECEMBER | MISTLETOE

Mistletoe is a mysterious plant – it sprouts from within the branches of fruit trees and forms a circular mass of green among the bare stems, as if the parent tree has become possessed. It speaks still of the continuity of life, vigorous and green when nearly everything else seems to have died or lies asleep.

It is scarce in the wild, unless you live in the old orchard-growing areas of western England, but it turns up in markets at this time of year so that you can bring a sprig of two into the house.

The sticky white mistletoe berries are one of the original fertility symbols and they rely on a few of our visiting birds to spread the plant from tree to tree. It is only the thrushes that seem to like eating them: redwings and fieldfares love them and, of course, they give a name to the handsome mistle thrush.

19 DECEMBER | YEW

The last of the wreath-making materials come from the yew that grows in the front garden.

Yew trees are some of the oldest living things on Earth. It is said that 'most trees look older than they are, except for yews, which are even older than they look.'

Dozens of ancient churchyard trees predate the church beside them. They have long been associated with sacred ground – another of the evergreens with magical powers, and they do have a hint of immortality – and they can regenerate even if chopped back, blown over or split by a gale.

I just need a few of this year's branches for the wreath. I will avoid the red berries surrounding the poisonous seeds and leave them for the birds that seem immune to them.

20 DECEMBER | WOODLAND

'No man is an island, entire of itself; every man is a piece of the continent, a part of the main'. ('No Man is an Island', John Donne, 1624.)

Woods in winter can be the quietest of places.

Yet, the stillness should not be mistaken for inactivity. We are beginning to understand that woods are more like a city than we could ever have imagined. Beneath the soil lies a huge volume of fungi – linking together the trees into the 'wood wide web'.

We have long known that trees and fungi work together to exchange sugars for minerals and that the woodland soil is full of fungal filaments as a result. We now know that these connect trees together into a giant network. And there is more … trees secretly talk to each other underground.

I have always wondered why some trees in woodland seem to die so suddenly. It now seems that sick trees pass their nutrients to neighbouring trees and 'sacrifice' themselves. Similarly adult trees can give nutrients to younger trees using fungal connections.

It now seems that information can flow along these fungal network cables, conveying information about pest attacks, or perhaps even the footfall of a visitor. The wood is behaving a little like a brain.

21 DECEMBER | WINTER SOLSTICE

For those of us who struggle with winter, today is a big day.

Tomorrow, and for the next six months, the light will start to win the battle over the dark at the rate of a minute or two each day. The Northern Hemisphere is slowly tilting back towards the sun. Spring is over the horizon.

In ancient Rome this was Saturnalia – 'the best of times', according to Catullus. For us this is also the season of parties and gifts. Christmas is still a few days away, but I think that we will emulate an Iranian tradition on the longest night of the year – gather some friends for food, drink and conversation.

22 DECEMBER | RED-LEGGED PARTRIDGE

… and a partridge in a pear tree.

Partridges are around in abundance at this time of year. Along with pheasants, they are released in their millions to the countryside each winter. Red-legged partridges (nicknamed 'Frenchmen' where I live) have grey bodies with bold black stripes and a white throat. They have a straight, humming flight with a few quick flaps and a glide.

The French name for partridge is 'un perdrix' – which if you pronounce it sounds very like 'pear tree' – giving rise to the suspicion that the song itself is a mistranslation from the French. From here on, I shall try singing 'a partridge and another partridge'.

23 DECEMBER | FINCH FLOCK

'December 23, 1770 – Linnets flock & haunt the oat stubbles & pease-fields.'

A wild winter day. Wind whistles through the window frames and the remaining leaves march circles across the grass.

It's time for a walk. The beech trees in the wood are clattering like a drum section, so it's a day for an open path, gulping for air as the wind greedily steals my breath.

Hopping between the field edge stubble and the trees is a cluster of birds: a winter finch flock. It is too grey to see much more than the odd flash of white among the brown wings, but I know that there will probably be several types of bird in here: linnets, chaffinches, buntings and perhaps a skylark as well.

There might be some winter visitors from the east in here too – bramblings perhaps, which look like a chaffinch that has been in the washing machine.

You could spend all day hunting for a finch flock and not find one. Leave them as something unlooked-for – a surprising early Christmas gift.

24 DECEMBER | PEAR

By the cricket ground a single hedgerow pear tree marks where once the orchard stood. The tree is tall and leans slightly, with dark bark fractured into squares.

This is a 'perry' pear, once grown to produce little pears that were crushed to make sweet pear cider. This was once the currency of these parts. The man who dug the water supply to the pavilion a century ago did the task in exchange for a bed for three weeks and an unlimited supply of cider.

Pear trees have wonderful pale wood that is good for carving, but while I love the tree I have never quite got to like the fruit. There are no partridges in sight either.

25 DECEMBER | ON THE SUBJECT OF GIFTS

This year I remembered to give some deferred nature gifts for Christmas. Here is my list:

Some snowdrop and aconite bulbs for January.
A fruit tree in February – you might like a dwarf plum in a pot.
A bottle of sake to drink under the March cherry blossom.
A house martin nest box for our April arrivals.
A promise to take you to visit a bluebell-clad island in May.
A picnic rug for a midsummer solstice party.
Some wildflower seed to make a bee-dazed July.
A neat wooden box for a seaside pebble collection.
A pot of damson jam from the September harvest.
A little set of oil paints in October tones.
A hedgerow tree for anyone who wants one in November.
A December notebook for the year ahead.

26 DECEMBER | WREN

How did we get to Boxing Day before mentioning the little lucky wren?

These are our shortest (and almost our smallest) birds but they are here all year, and should be as close a companion as your local robin. They have round brown bodies, little upright tails and an explosive song that is improbably loud for such a tiny bird.

They eat insects and love to get to the places that other birds can't reach – underneath a piece of decking, in the cracks in the wall or the holes between.

They get a mention today because this is the date of the ancient tradition of 'hunting the wren', which is believed to date back to the Celts and beyond and still is part of the culture of the Isle of Man and parts of France.

It's hard work finding a wren on a cold winter day, because they like tucking up together in a shared roost, just like families squashed on a Boxing Day sofa.

They are particularly fond of nest boxes for this purpose and there is a record of 61 wrens snuggling top to tail in a winter Norfolk nest box. If you think your living room is crammed at Christmas, think again.

27 DECEMBER | A DAILY NATURE RUN

After 48 hours of food, I have the urge to take a slow, heavy Christmas run. It took me a while to learn that I didn't like running on roads, but running in nature is a different thing all together. Not only can you keep an eye out for plants and birds, but if you see something interesting then you have an ironclad excuse to take a breather.

My running route drops into the valley where the stream runs, still flanked with watercress even at this time of year. The days have imperceptibly started to get longer again and in the woods I sense that the winter sleep of the trees is giving way to wakefulness.

On the track lie fragments of hazelnut and the crushed, hairy cases of beech nuts. There are one or two insects above the water. The path back up is slippery with mud where the winter storms have drained away. There is no hint of warmth in the air yet, but soon the year will turn.

28 DECEMBER | ROBIN

The Christmas cards are full of robins, breasts stained with symbolic blood. The robin's nest from last spring lies empty in the little open sided nest box by the shed.

Yet step outside with a tray full of crumbs and like as not a robin will appear, head cocked sideways in an amused way, as if to say 'get on with it and get back inside'.

It's not too long now before they will be back at their territorial tussle, puffing out their breast at any intruder and chasing them as they fly off to show who is the boss.

29 DECEMBER | PLANNING SOME NATURE PARTIES

It's time to come out. Loving nature is not something to be embarrassed about, it is part of the human condition.

So, to encourage myself I am marking out next year's calendar with a list of things to do. I am going to be micro-ambitious.

I will definitely be inviting some people for a drink under the cherry blossom in the street. I am going to make a fuss about the first stick-carrying rook and my own brimstone day.

This year, I am going to drag the children out of bed at 4am for an hour to listen to the dawn chorus. In exchange we will stay up until midnight playing games on midsummer night.

There is cordial to make and apples to press. I have a list of little nature projects for the house: a miniature fruit tree, a log pile, a tiny pond, a ledge for house martins.

30 DECEMBER | LIST OF THINGS TO LEARN NEXT YEAR

'To see a world in a grain of sand. And a heaven in a wild flower, Hold infinity in the palm of your hand. And eternity in an hour.' ('Auguries of Innocence', William Blake, *c.*1803.)

There is more in nature than any of us will ever know. Even now we are still finding new species even in this busy little island. Blake invites us to rejoice in this rather than be daunted by it.

This book is a starting point – you will never end the process of learning about nature, so you might as well just begin. Don't worry about getting things wrong: science occasionally moves the goalposts anyway as more things are discovered.

Animals, butterflies and birds are a good place to start. Over time you can learn most of the species that occur here. Most trees are fairly easy too once you get your eye in.

There are a lot more moths and fungi (a few thousand), but you can quite quickly become familiar with the common ones. Next year I am going to learn my bumble bees. There are not that many varieties and I am becoming very fond of them.

Mosses, grasses, liverworts, flies and beetles are in the more difficult bracket – but over time you can become a specialist if the mood takes you.

If you do one thing as you learn then make sure that you are generous with what you know – praise people for what they know rather than pointing out what they don't.

31 DECEMBER | NOTICING NATURE

It's a time for reflection and looking forward. This year has reminded me that some of the simplest things in life are the hardest to do.

The act of noticing things is one of those. As soon as you become familiar with something then it's easy to stop looking at it. I have to repeat to myself: notice, look closely, be curious.

So, the year turns and nature's cycle repeats: Always the same, yet never the quite the same.

I have a calendar filled with things to do. Tomorrow is the day to head out to the warmest bank I can find to see if the snowdrops are pushing through the grass. I will keep an eye out for the young hazel catkins taking shape on the hedge as I pass. There may even be an early hellebore flower …

ABOUT THE AUTHOR

Andy Beer grew up on a 60s housing estate on the edge of Highworth in Wiltshire. He spent his childhood roaming the surrounding fields and catching butterflies in overgrown hedgerows. At the age of seventeen a summer spent under the huge skies of the island of Fair Isle unleashed his lifelong love of nature. He is an environmental scientist by training and spends as much of his National Trust working life as possible outdoors. A voracious reader of naturalists from Gilbert White to Aldo Leopold, Andy Beer is prone to distraction with whatever is happening inside his head or outside the window, to the exasperation of his partner, Heather, and his two children. *Everyday Nature* is his first book.

ACKNOWLEDGEMENTS

This book is the work of an amateur naturalist and an even more amateur writer. It draws humbly on the writings of some brilliant ecologists and communicators: Richard Mabey, John Lewis-Stempel, Dave Goulson, Stephen Moss, Roger Deakin, Matthew Oates, Robert Macfarlane, Will Cohu, Isabella Tree, Gilbert White, Thomas Hardy, John Clare, Laurie Lee, Edward Thomas, Anne Brontë, William Shakespeare, Richard Jefferies.

I am grateful to the following organisations for inspiration and fact-checking: National Trust, Wildfowl and Wetlands Trust, British Trust for Ornithology, The Royal Society for the Protection of Birds, Plantlife, Woodland Trust, Buglife, Froglife, Butterfly Conservation, *BBC Wildlife*, *New Scientist*, *The Guardian*, University College London, Natural History Museum.

Dozens of people helped with content for the book, including Kathy and Nigel Gilks, Matt Darby, Harry Bowell, Mike Innerdale, Gordon and Prith Bell, Tim Parsonson, Mark and Anna Esler, Will and Frances Ridsdill Smith, members of the Gretton cider-pressing gang and many others.

Thanks to my friends at Winchcombe Running Club for putting up with owl-spotting and interruptions for meteors – particularly Nick Spice for his relentless encouragement and Colin Tilley Loughrey for the design advice.

Thank you to Mum and Dad, Susan, Richard and the rest of the family for all the moral support and ideas (and sorry in advance, Sue, about the pigeon references).

Thank you to my friends at the National Trust and, in particular my team – Ben, Lucy, Louise, Jo, Emma, Elie, Alan and Clair – for putting up with my complaints about writing.

Thanks to Peter Taylor, Nicola Newman and the publishing team at Pavilion Books, and to Lesley Buckingham for her beautiful illustrations; to Katie Bond for constant inspiration and encouragement; and to Carl Hawke and Daniel Dodd for taking the time to read the manuscript and provide insightful comments.

Finally, thanks to Heather, Tom and Roo for putting up with endless walks, playing the piano to owls and hearing the same stories several times over.

INDEX